SPIRIT OF THE MACHINE
TECHNOLOGY AS AN INSPIRATION IN ARCHITECTURAL DESIGN

Robert Kronenburg

WILEY-ACADEMY

For your future: Anna, Alex, Ella

First published in Great Britain in 2001 by
WILEY-ACADEMY

A division of
JOHN WILEY & SONS
Baffins Lane
Chichester
West Sussex
PO19 1UD

ISBN: 0-471-978-604

Copyright © 2001 Robert Kronenburg. All rights reserved. No part of this publication may be reproduced, stored in a retrieval system, or transmitted, in any form or by means, electronic, mechanical, photocopying, recording, scanning or otherwise, except under the terms of the Copyright Designs and Patents Act 1988 or under the terms of a license issued by the Copyright Licensing Agency, 90 Tottenham Court Road, London, UK, W1P 9HE, without the permission in writing of the publisher or the copyright owner.

Other Wiley Editorial offices
New York • Weinheim • Brisbane • Singapore • Toronto

Printed and bound in Italy.

Cover: Ramsgate airport proposal, 1937, from the *Architectural Review*, July 1937.

Frontispiece: Symbol of the city – car park and office building spanning the motorway entering The Hague, Netherlands. The Malietoren by Benthem and Crowel, 1991–96.

CONTENTS

Acknowledgements		vi
Chronology		vii
Foreword		1
Part 1	**Technology, Architecture and Meaning**	9
	Controlling technology	12
	The role of contemporary architecture	20
	The technological characteristics of architectural form	26
	Humanistic associations with architecture	31
Part 2	**Themes in Technologically Inspired Architecture**	47
	Pop architecture	48
	Pure architecture	55
	Organic architecture	62
	Tectonic architecture	67
Part 3	**The Purpose of Technology in Architecture**	79
	Vernacular architecture - holistic design	91
	Alternative architecture - responsive design	96
	Intuitive architecture - releasing creativity	100
Selected Bibliography		113

ACKNOWLEDGEMENTS

In a work that has taken some seven years to come to gestation there are many whose help and influence must be acknowledged. The explorations for this book first began as a lecture and seminar series that I prepared for a United States Fulbright Foundation fellowship in 1994 and the benefits of this initial study and research period were very important. Further support was provided specifically for this work by the Graham Foundation in Chicago allowing primary research to be carried out abroad. A residential fellowship at St. John's College, Oxford enabled valuable work to be done at the Bodleian Library. In addition I must thank the many practitioners with whom I have discussed these issues from time to time, in particular, Todd Dalland, Mark Fisher, Nicholas Goldsmith, Richard Horden, Michael Knight, Ian Liddell, and the students of Kansas State University, Liverpool John Moores University, and the University of Liverpool with whom I have been fortunate to work during this period. I must also thank my publisher Maggie Toy for her patience and continuing support for a project that lasted longer than any of us anticipated.

ILLUSTRATION ACKNOWLEDGEMENTS

The author and publishers would like to thank those who have kindly permitted the use of images in the illustration of this book. Attempts have been made to locate all the sources of illustrations to obtain full reproduction rights, but in the very few instances where this process has failed to find the copyright holder, apologies are offered. In the case of an error, correction would be welcomed.

Airbus and Computer Graphics i3m, 11. Alfons Dlugosz, Wielicka Magnum Sal., Arkady, Warsaw, 93. Architectural Review 1937, cover. Atasushi Nakamichi, Nacasa and Partners Inc., Tokyo, 24. Axel Thallemer (Prof. Dipl.-Ing.), Head of Festo Corporate Design, 3.1 - 3.7. B. Shapiro, 103. Bildarchiv Foto Marburg, 26, 56. British Columbia Archives (call number D-08290) Pacific Archives Northwest, 87. Buckminster Fuller Estate, Sebastopol, CA, (courtesy of), 71, 82. Bui/ding, 15. Butler Manufacturing Company, 83. Clacton Public Library, 99. Donald J. Bush, Tempe, Arizona, 46. Engineering, 16. Ernst Haeckel Haus, Jena, 28. Fotofolio, New York, 3. Frank Lloyd Wright Foundation, The drawings of Frank Lloyd Wright are Copyright 1994, 2001 The Frank Lloyd Wright Foundation, Scottsdale, AZ, 38. Fransechini, N., Pichon,J.M., Blanes, C. (1992)'From InsectVisiontoRobotVision', Phil. Trans. Roy. Soc. B337, 283-294., 29. FTL Happold, 1 06, 1 07. Gabinetto Fotografico Nazionale, 9. General Motors Corporation, 45. Georg Wegner, 94. Her Majestys Stationary Office, 85. Illustrated London News Picture Library, 1 4. Jocelyne van den Bossche, 78. John W. R. Taylor and Michael J.H.Taylor, 22. J0rn Utzon, 104. Jose Ortiz Echague, 20. Keystone Press Agency, 86. Loos Archive Albertina, Vienna, 55. Lucia Eames/Eames Office 2001 © (www.eamesoffice.com), 72. Lucia Eames/photo by Tim Street-Porter 1997/2001 ©, 73. M.F.Ashby, 84. Margaret Nissen, 89. Musee d l'Homme, photograph B. Dupaigne, 95. Museum fur Volkerkunde, Basel, 88. NASA, 12. Nicholas Grimshaw and Partners, 77. Patrick Shanahan, 100. Peabody Trust and Cartwright Pickard Architects, 1.1 - 1.8. Peter CookNIEW, 79. Peter Crawley, 96. Popperfoto, 105. Random House, Jacket cover from 1961 paperback edition of 2001:A Space Odysseyby Arthur C. Clarke published by Arrow. Used by permission of the Random House Group Limited, 1. Reto Fuhrer, 90. Richard Rogers Partnership, 32. Robert Kronenburg 33, frontispiece, 4, 6, 7, 8, 10, 17, 18, 21, 25, 27, 30, 31, 33, 34, 35, 36, 39, 42, 43, 44, 48, 50, 51, 52, 57, 58, 59, 60, 61, 63, 65, 66, 68, 69, 70, 74, 75, 76, 80, 91, 92, 97, 101, 102, 109, 110, 2,1-2.6. Shigeru Ban Architect, 2.7, 2.8. Stephanie Bunn 1995, 13. Tezuka productions, Hyogo Phoenix Plan, 5. Thomas A. Heinz, 37. Time Warner Inc. ©, 2. Turner Entertainment Co. All Rights Reserved © 1949, 47. Warner bros Inc. 1989 ©, 23. William F. Winter, Jr., photographer, 19. William Morris Gallery, London E17, 49.

CHRONOLOGY

Year	Society	Architecture	Technology
1900	Sigmund Freud's *The Interpretation of Dreams* published John Ruskin dies The first car race ever held between Paris and Lyon	Edwin Lutyens' house The Deanery, Sonning, UK C.F.A. Voysey's house The Orchard, Chorley Wood, UK	Quantum theory established by Max Planck Marconi's patent for the tuned radio transmitter First gramophone records marketed
1901	The Nobel Prize is awarded for the first time	Louis Sullivan's Carson Pirie Scott Department Store, begun in Chicago	
1902	Aswan Dam opens revolutionising Egypt's economy	Herman Muthesias' *Das Englishe Haus* published	
1903		Architects Elzner and Anderson, and engineer E.L. Ransome build the 16-storey reinforced concrete Ingall's Building in Cincinnati, USA	Orville and Wilbur Wright make first flight by a powered heavier-than-air aircraft in Kittyhawk, South Carolina, USA
1904		John Alexander Brodie, City Engineer of Liverpool, builds the first housing made of prefabricated reinforced concrete panel construction	
1905		Otto Wagner's Post Office Savings Bank, Vienna, Austria	Albert Einstein establishes the theory of relativity Softwood based plywood first introduced
1906	San Francisco earthquake and fire	Charley Mewes and Arthur Davis build The Ritz, London, the first large steel frame building in Britain	
1907	British Women's Suffrage Movement storms the Houses of Parliament Pablo Picasso paints *Les Demoiselles d'Avignon*		August and Louis Lumière invent autochrome colour photography process Einstein creates the equation that describes the equivalence of mass and energy: $E=mc^2$
1908			Tungsten filament incandescent lamps introduced Ford Model T car introduced
1909	Louis Bleriot flies across the English Channel National Associations for the Advancement of Coloured People (NAACP) founded in the USA Robert Peary reaches the North Pole	Peter Behrens' AEG Turbine Hall, Berlin Futurist Manifesto published in *Le Figaro*	
1910	Igor Stravinsky's *Firebird* first performed Murderer Dr Crippen caught on transatlantic liner due to Marconi wireless message	Adolf Loos' Steiner House, Vienna, Austria Adolf Loos' essay *Arkitecture* published	Edison invents 'kinetophone' system for talking pictures
1911	Amundsen reaches South Pole, Scott dies in the attempt Greenwich Mean Time becomes an international standard	Walter Gropius and Adolf Meyer's Fagus Factory, Alfeld-an-der-Leine, Germany	The aeroplane first used in combat
1912	Warner Brothers, Fox, and Universal film studios founded in Hollywood *Titanic* sinks in North Atlantic		Stainless steel invented
1913	Panama Canal opens	Cass Gilbert's Woolworth Building completed in New York, tallest building in the world at 232 metres	First assembly line production system introduced by Ford Niels Bohr develops the theory of atomic structure

Year	Society	Architecture	Technology
1914	First World War begins, USA declares neutrality	42 storey, steel framed L.C. Smith Building built in Seattle, USA	
1915	Passenger ship *Lusitania* sunk by German U-boat		Einstein establishes the general theory of relativity First US transcontinental telephone call between New York and San Francisco
1916	Easter Rising in Dublin Margaret Singer opens first birth control clinic in New York The Battle of the Somme, over a million men die in 142 days		
1917	First commercial jazz recording, USA October Revolution in Russia USA enters the First World War	Tony Garnier's book *Une Cité Industrielle* published	
1918	World's first air mail service starts in USA Women gain the vote in Britain Armistice signed; First World War ends		Sonar invented
1919	Women granted political equality in Germany John Alcock and Arthur Whitten-Brown fly the Atlantic non-stop in a Vickers Vimy bomber	Walter Gropius appointed first director of the Bauhaus Tatlin designs the the Third International unbuilt Monument to Communist Congress, Moscow Eric Mendelsohn's Einstein Tower, Berlin begun	First helicopter flight
1920	Prohibition introduced in USA Nazi Party formed in Germany Women gain the vote in USA		First commercial radio broadcast Discovery of the neutron
1921	Creation of the Irish Free State		
1922	British Broadcasting Company founded Howard Carter discovers the tomb of Tutankhamen in Egypt	Adolf Loos' entry for the Chicago Tribune Building competition; Raymond Hood and John Mead Howells win with a Gothic design	
1923	Tokyo earthquake and fire	Le Corbusier's book *Vers une Architecture* published in Paris (English language edition published 1927)	The astronomer Hubble discovers another galaxy beyond the Milky Way
1924	George Gershwin's *Rhapsody in Blue* first performed	Gerrit Thomas Rietveld's Schröder House, Utrecht, Holland	Production line plate glass first manufactured at the Ford Factory in the USA
1925	Stalin comes to power in the USSR	Le Corbusier's mass-produced concrete housing at Pessac, Bordeaux, France Exposition International des Arts Décoratifs et Industriels Modernes, Paris, Le Corbusier's *'Pavilion de L'Esprit Nouveau'*	
1926	Fritz Lang's film *Metropolis* released Josephine Baker tours Europe British General Strike	New Bauhaus opens in Dessau, Germany	First television transmission by John Logie Baird in the UK First liquid fuelled rocket developed
1927	Charles Lindbergh flies non-stop from New York to Paris Airship *Graf Zeppelin* completes journey around the world in 21 days	Le Corbusier's Villa Savoie, Poissy, Paris begun R. Buckminster Fuller designs Dymaxian House in the USA	

Year	Society	Architecture	Technology
1928	Henry Ford's book *My Philosophy of Industry* published Five year industrialisation plan introduced in the USSR Mickey Mouse appears for the first time	Le Corbusier, Berlage, Rietveld, Stam, Haering, Chareau, Moser, Sartoris and others meet at the Castle of La Sarraz, Lake Geneva to establish CIAM William Van Allen's Chrysler Building, New York, begun, completed 1931	Alexander Fleming discovers penicillin
1929	Wall Street Crash, USA Worldwide economic depression takes hold First commercial television broadcasts by the BBC First talking motion picture *The Jazz Singer*	Mies van der Rohe's German Pavilion at the Barcelona Expo completed	
1930	Sigmung Freud writes *Civilisation and its Discontents*	Owen Williams' Dry Process Building, Boots opens Factory, Beeston, Nottingham, UK	
1931		Le Corbusier's *Palais des Soviets* project, Moscow	
1932		Sydney Harbour Bridge opens Philip Johnson and H.R. Hitchcock exhibition and book *The International Style*, New York	Polyamide fibres (nylon) developed
1933	Adolf Hitler becomes Chancellor of Germany Franklin D. Roosevelt becomes president of the USA and introduces the New Deal		Synthetic wood glues introduced in Germany, leading to mass-production of plywood and wood fibre products Polyethylene (the most common plastic) discovered by ICI in England
1934	The Long March (completed 1935) in China helps Mao Tse-Tung to power American gangsters Bonnie Parker and Clyde Barrow shot dead	Erich Mendelsohn and Serge Chermayeff's De La Warr Pavilion, Bexhill, East Sussex, UK Bertold Lubetkin and Tecton's Penguin Pool, London Zoo	
1935		Frank Lloyd Wright's house, Falling Water, Pennsylvania, USA Greenbelt policy formed to prevent urban sprawl in the UK Crystal Palace destroyed by fire	Radar invented by Robert Watson-Watt
1936	Charlie Chaplin's film *Modern Times* released Spanish Civil War begins Alexander Korda's film, scripted by H.G. Wells, *Things to Come* is released		Olympic Games in Germany televised
1937		Albert Speer's neo-classical master plan for Berlin	Golden Gate Bridge, San Francisco completed Whittle designs the jet gas turbine engine in England German airship *Hindenburg* crashes on landing in USA
1938	Orson Welles' radio play of H.G. Wells' book *The War of the Worlds* generates panic in USA 'Kristallnacht' widespread violence against Jews in Germany		Otto Hahn splits the atom *The Mallard* reaches 126 mph near Peterborough, UK, the highest speed ever achieved by a steam locomotive
1939	New York World's Fair featuring Norman Bel Geddes *Futurama* exhibit for General Motors Spanish Civil War ends Second World War begins		Tacoma Narrow Bridge built (collapses 1940)

Year	Society	Architecture	Technology
1940	Dunkirk evacuation, Battle of Britain and the London Blitz		
1941	Orson Welles' film *Citizen Kane* released Japanese attack Pearl Harbour and America joins the Second World War		The 'Manhattan Project' for Atomic Weapons Research begins in the USA First programme controlled computer developed by German, Konrad Zuse
1942	Battle of El-Alamein, North Africa	Frank Lloyd Wright designs Guggenheim Museum, New York (built 1957–60)	Penicillin introduced Enrico Fermi constructs the first atomic pile in New York Uranium atom split in Chicago, USA The first A4 rocket (known to the Allies as the V2) launched in Peenemunde, Germany
1943	RAF's Dambuster air raid on the Ruhr Valley		
1944	D-Day, invasion of mainland Europe by Allied forces		
1945	United Nations founded by charter Atomic bombs dropped on Hiroshima and Nagasaki by the USA Second World War ends: Germany surrenders 8 May, Japan surrenders 14 August	Mies van der Rohe's Farnsworth House, Plano, USA Alison and Peter Smithson's Hunstanton School begun (completed 1954)	The first successful test of the atomic bomb in Nevada, USA, 16 July
1946	Regular transatlantic passenger air service introduced Nationalisation begins in Britain	R. Buckminster Fuller's prototype Wichita House completed by Beech Aircraft Company, USA Le Corbusier's Unité d'Habitation, Marseilles, France, begun (completed 1952) Alvar Aalto's Baker Dormitory, MIT, Cambridge, Mass., USA	
1947	Anne Frank's diary published in Holland Indian independence, partition follows	Charles and Ray Eames' House, Pacific Palisades, California, begun (completed 1948)	Transistor invented Chuck Yeager breaks the sound barrier in the Bell Aircraft Company's X1 rocket plane
1948	Berlin Air Lift begins (concludes 1949)	Mies van der Rohe's Lake Shore Drive Apartments, Chicago begun (completed 1951) R. Buckminster Fuller builds his first large scale geodesic dome	Volkswagon Beetle goes into production Norbert Wiener's book *Cybernetics: or Control and Communication in the Animal and the Machine* is published
1949	King Vidor's film of Ayn Rand's novel *The Fountainhead* released Communist People's Republic of China declared by Mao Tse-Tung George Orwell's book *1984* published	Philip Johnson's Glass House, Connecticut, USA	
1950	Korean War begins	Le Corbusier's Notre Dame du Haut, Ronchamp, France begun (completed 1955)	
1951		Festival of Britain on London's South Bank Le Corbusier begins design work on the government buildings at Chandigarh, India (completed 1965)	First British nuclear reactor goes on-line
1952	Kinsey report on sexuality released in the USA Eva Peron dies in Argentina	First Holiday Inn built in USA	Experiments leading to the development of the float glass production method begun by the Pilkington Factory, UK

Year	Society	Architecture	Technology
1953	Sir Edmund Hillary and Sherpa Tenzing Norgay climb Mount Everest Stalin dies China begins its first five-year plan Elizabeth II coronation Korean War ends		Martin Heidegger delivers his lecture *The Question Concerning Technology* in Bremen, Germany Francis Crick and James Watson propose the double helix as a model for the DNA molecule
1954	Bill Haley and the Comets release *Rock Around the Clock* Henry Matisse dies		Polio vaccine developed by Jonas Salk First commercial transistor radio
1955	Clean Air Act passed in Britain to combat pollution Albert Einstein dies Disneyland opens in Anaheim, California		
1956	The Suez Crisis	Eero Saarinen's TWA terminal buildings begun, New York, (completed 1962) Jørn Utzon's Sydney Opera House begun (completed 1973)	First practical video tape recorder developed by Ampex in the USA
1957	Treaty of Rome establishes the European Economic Community Jack Kerouac's book *On the Road* published	CLASP (Construction of Local Authorities Special Commission) established to industrialise construction of school buildings	*Sputnik I* satellite launched National Aeronautics and Space Administration (NASA) founded in the USA
1958	Campaign for Nuclear Disarmament (CND) founded		
1959	Cuban Revolution, Fidel Castro takes power		The integrated circuit invented by Kirby and Noyce
1960	John F. Kennedy elected president of the USA 'Sharpville Massacre' at a civil rights demonstration in South Africa	Robert and Denise Venturis' Guild House, Philadelphia, USA, begun (completed 1963)	First laser built by American scientist T.H. Maiman Contraceptive pill introduced
1961	Berlin Wall built 'Bay of Pigs' abortive US-backed invasion of Cuba		Soviet cosmonaut Yuri Gagarin orbits the Earth
1962	Rachel Carson's book *Silent Spring* published concerning the danger of pesticides Marilyn Monroe dies Cuban missile crisis	Sir Basil Spence's Coventry Cathedral consecrated	John Glenn becomes the first American in space
1963	USA's involvement with the Vietnam War formalised John F. Kennedy assassinated in Dallas, USA The Beatles release *She Loves You*		*Telstar*, the first communications satellite launched
1964	Nelson Mandela sentenced to life imprisonment in South Africa	Bernard Rudofsky's *Architecture without Architects* exhibition and book	First automatic, computer controlled, flexible manufacturing system developed by the Molins Company, London
1965	Marshall McLuhan's book *Understanding Media: The Extensions of Man* published Le Corbusier (Charles Edward Jeanneret) dies aged 77		

Year	Society	Architecture	Technology
1966	Barbara Ward's book *Spaceship Earth* published Gene Rodenberry's television series *Star Trek* premiers	Robert and Denise Venturis' book *Complexity and Contradiction in Architecture* published. Aldo Rossi's book *The Architecture of the City* published	
1967	The Beatles *Sgt Peppers' Lonely Hearts Club Band* record released Cultural Revolution in China		Heart transplant completed by Christiaan Barnard Electronic quartz wristwatch developed
1968	Stanley Kubrick's film co-scripted by Arthur C. Clarke, *2001: A Space Odyssey* released Martin Luther King assassinated Racial discrimination outlawed in Britain Richard Nixon elected US president	Mies van der Rohe's Neue Nationalgalerie, Berlin	ARPA-Net, precurser of the Internet, developed
1969	Woodstock music festival	Mies van der Rohe dies	First Moon landing by *Apollo 11*, 20 July, nearly a third of the entire world population watches on television as Neil Armstrong steps on to the Moon First flights by supersonic airliner Concorde, Bristol, UK
1970	The Beatles split	Alternative building handbook *Domebook* first published in California, USA	IBM develops the floppy disk
1971	Victor Papanek's book *Design for the Real World* published Greenpeace founded	Renzo Piano and Richard Rogers' Beaubourg Centre, Paris begun (completed 1977) Arne Jacobsen dies	First commercially available personal computer Intel develops the micro-processor
1972	Bloody Sunday in Northern Ireland USA leaves Vietnam	Norman Foster's Willis-Faber and Dumas building, Ipswich, UK, begun (completed 1975) Italo Calvino's book *Invisible Cities* published Frei Otto's Munich Olympic Stadium, Germany	Chaos theory named by James Yorke based on earlier work by Edward Lorenz Brain scanner invented by Godfrey Hounsfield at the EMI Company, UK Last manned Moon landing
1973	E.F. Schumaker's book *Small is Beautiful* published Britain joins the EEC		
1974	Watergate scandal, US president Nixon resigns	Norman Foster's Sainsbury Centre for the Visual Arts, Norwich, UK begun (completed 1977) Skidmore Owings and Merrill's, Sears Tower, Chicago, tallest building in the world at 442 metres	
1975	Microsoft founded by Bill Gates		Benoit Mandelbrot coins the term 'fractal' to describe endlessly repeating geometric shapes
1976	Apple founded by Steve Jobs and Stephen Wozniak Sex Pistols release *Anarchy in the UK*	Denis Lasdun's National Theatre, London, opens	
1977	George Lucas' film *Star Wars* released	Cedric Price's Interaction Centre, Kentish Town, London	
1978		Rem Koolhaas' book *Delirious New York* published	
1979	James Lovelock's book *Gaia: A New Look at Life on Earth* published	Norman Foster's Hong Kong Shanghai Bank, Hong Kong begun (completed 1985)	English Channel crossed by a US-made man-powered aircraft Three Mile Island nuclear disaster, US

Year	Society	Architecture	Technology
1980	Formation of 'Solidarity' trade union in Poland John Lennon murdered	*Presence of the Past* exhibition, Venice, Paris and San Francisco containing building designs by leading post-modern designers James Stirling's Staatsgalerie, Stuttgart, Germany begun (completed 1983)	Sony 'Walkman' launched
1981	Acquired Immune Deficiency Sydrome (AIDS) officially recognised		*Columbia* Space Shuttle reusable spacecraft first launched The Humber Bridge, world's longest suspension bridge, completed
1982	Ridley Scott's film *Bladerunner* released Falklands War between Britain and Argentina	Richard Horden's Yacht House, New Forest, UK	
1983	Polish activist Lech Walesa wins the Nobel Peace Prize President Reagan initiates the Strategic Defence Initiative (SDI) nicknamed 'Star Wars' after the 1977 film	Richard Meier's High Museum, Atlanta, USA	
1984	Renewed anti-nuclear protests in UK Bhopal Chemical pollution disaster, India	Bernard Tschumi's Parc de la Villette, Paris Richard Meier's Applied Art Museum, Frankfurt, Germany	Genetically engineered mouse 'oncomouse' developed for cancer research at the Harvard Medical School, USA
1985	Coal miners' strike, UK Mikhail Gorbachev becomes Soviet leader Live Aid	IBA housing projects, Berlin	
1986	Nintendo craze begins	Richard Rogers' Lloyd's Building, City of London	Space Shuttle *Challenger* explodes on take-off Chernobyl nuclear power station accident in the USSR
1987		Jean Nouvel's Arab World Institute, Paris	Glass fibre optic cable laid across Atlantic New world record for space endurance on Soviet space station *Mir*, 326 days
1988	Pan Am flight 103 destroyed by terrorist bomb and crashes on Lockerbie, Scotland	Tadao Ando's Chapel on the Water, Tomamu, Japan Norman Foster's Stanstead Airport Terminal Building, UK	
1989	Supertanker *Exxon Valdez* deposits oil slick off Alaska Berlin Wall destroyed	Pete Eisenman's Wexner Center for the Visual Arts, Columbus, Ohio, USA Johan Otto Van Spreckelsen and Paul Andrew's Grande Arch de la Defence, Paris I.M. Pei's Louvre Pyramid, Paris completed	
1990	Nelson Mandela released in South Africa BSE fears increase in Britain Iraq invades Kuwait Collapse of USSR		World Wide Web software introduced to make Internet available to a mass market Hubble space telescope is launched and a lens fault is found
1991	Gulf War Soviet Union disbanded into separate states		
1992	War in Bosnia begins Bill Clinton elected US president	Nicholas Grimshaw's British Pavilion at Expo '92 Seville, Spain	

Year	Society	Architecture	Technology
1993		Zaha Hadid's Vitra Fire Station, Weil am Rhein, Germany	SDI abandoned
1994	Nelson Mandela becomes South Africa's first black president O.J. Simpson 'media' trial British National Lottery begins Russian Chechen conflict begins		Channel Tunnel between UK and France inaugurated
1995	Giant earthquake hits Kobe, Japan	Rem Koolhas' book *S.M.L.X.L* published	Scientists accelerate particle beyond the speed of light
1996	Government admits link between BSE and CJD diseases	Reproduction of Shakespeare's Globe Theatre opens in London Cesar Pelli's Petronas Towers, Kuala Lumpur, completed; the tallest building in the world at 452 metres	TWA airliner explodes off north west coast of USA due to static electricity in fuel tank
1997	Labour government under Tony Blair comes to power in Britain Princess Diana killed	Office for Metropolitan Architecture's Educatorium Building, Utrecht, Netherlands Mecanoo's Delft University of Technology library constructed, Netherlands	*Galileo* space probe makes close pass by Jupiter Chess grandmaster Gary Kasparov is beaten by computer 'Deep Blue'
1998	US President Clinton embroiled in sex scandals		Akalshi Kaikyo Bridge, Japan, completed, the longest suspension bridge in the world at 890 metres
1999	Single currency launched in Europe Columbia High School student massacre in USA NATO sends ground troops into Kosovo	Daniel Libeskind's Jewish Museum, Berlin, completed Norman Foster's Berlin Reichstag refurbishment completed Frank Gehry's Guggenheim Museum, Bilbao, Portugal, completed	Repaired Hubble space telescope discovers the oldest galaxy in the universe at 14.25 billion years old
2000	World governments fail to reach agreement over reduction in global warming emissions at meeting in the Hague Extensive floods in the UK	Shigeru Ban's recyclable Japan pavilion at Expo 2000 in Hannover, Germany Herzog and de Mueron's Tate Modern, London completed Foster, Caro and Ove Arup's Millennium footbridge across the Thames opens and closes Richard Rogers and Buro Happold's Millennium Dome, Greenwich, England completed	*Concorde* crashes for the first time in Paris

2001
a space odyssey

a novel by
Arthur C. Clarke

based on the screenplay by
Stanley Kubrick & Arthur C. Clarke

FOREWORD

My favourite film has remained the same since 1968 – Stanley Kubrick's *2001: A Space Odyssey*. I first saw it in my local cinema, a streamlined 1930's building situated on a hill top at the confluence of five roads at the sort of junction that is now a tangle of traffic lights. The building had recently been upgraded with the latest cinematic technology, 'Cinerama', an audio-visual *tour de force* with hi-fi surround sound and three synchronised projectors each showing a third of the whole image. *2001* was a wide-screen Super Panavision film with stereo – the cinema was packed each time I went to see it over those few weeks when I was fourteen years old.

2001 has remained at the top of my list throughout the intervening years though subsequent contenders have had to compete only with my memory . . . until I saw it again recently after buying a copy on DVD. At this recent viewing, sitting in my office in front of my computer, I was, however, surprised to find the experience quite depressing. Besides the sudden realisation that, without doubt, the title and themes of this film would in the year of its setting be appropriated to sell everything from furniture to hamburgers, it was equally certain that the predictions I was seeing would repeatedly be compared with the newly arrived reality.

The script is based on an idea by the scientist, science fiction writer and technological prophet Arthur C. Clarke. His short story *The Sentinel* described the discovery of an alien artefact found during an early space mission which alerted humanity to the certainty that it was not alone in the universe. Kubrick worked with Clarke to develop this scenario into a much grander tale that explored 'big' questions about human origins and what counts as intelligent life. At the beginning of the film proto-human apes are sparked into their next stage of development by contact with an alien object, a minimal technological slab made to pure mathematical proportions. One ape creates the first tool of our species, a bone used as a club, which is then cinematically transformed into a space ship as the story moves into the late twentieth century. This centre part of the film follows the journey of the interplanetary spacecraft *Discovery* to one of Jupiter's satellites (Saturn in the book, the destination was changed because Kubrick was unhappy with the special effects images of the planet's rings) which had been the target of a signal sent from the alien artefact found in Tycho crater on the Moon. However, the focus of this journey turns out to be not the approaching destination, but the omnipotent computer that controls the ship, which turns paranoid and kills all but one of the crew. The remaining astronaut eventually completes the journey and makes an astounding psychedelic journey through time and space which, however, answers few of the questions raised by the story.

Why discuss an old science fiction film at the outset of a book about architecture? Well, the reasons are of course partly personal: *2001* was one of those things that happened to me when I was young that invariably happens to all of us when we are coming to terms with the world we live in and what we are going to do there. It partly inspired the agenda I have engaged with for most of my working life – how technology impacts on the physical world, in particular the buildings, places and environments we make to support our activities. Apart from that, the perspective of that story and the way it was told tell us interesting things about the way technology was thought of in the 1960s compared with how we think of it now. I wrote earlier that I now find the film depressing – as I believe it still stands up as a masterpiece of the genre this is only partly true, but it is worth saying why. Though it was released a year before the *Apollo 11* mission successfully placed a man on the Moon, this film shows humankind as a confident space traveller. The Earth/space station shuttle is a commercial Pan Am flight, the space station itself is vast and beautiful, the moon station established and secure. It also shows the physical surroundings, telephones, furnishings, clothes, lighting, and especially the space vehicles which resemble buildings protecting the inhabitants from a particularly harsh environment, as an aesthetic integrated with innovative technology – the use of elegant Strauss waltzes to accompany the lovingly animated pirouettes of these craft has lost none of its power to convey a cinematic message about elegant, sophisticated technology.

As a boy I felt totally confident that within my lifetime I would see all this for real – if I had been a little older perhaps I would have been one of the thousands who phoned Pan Am to reserve a place for a future flight – and yet . . . though this book will be published in the year in which the film was set the predictions it made have for the most part not been achieved. In the 1960s Kubrick could create a believable story that expressed an intelligent confidence about the potential of technology and also looked beyond the gadgets and adventure to ideas about how it helped fulfil the ambitions of humanity. Some details do now look familiar: the computers that guide the craft between planets are remarkably similar to the glass cockpit in use in commercial and military aircraft and the video-phone is now becoming available to all via real time digital Internet video links. However, we now live in the age where humankind went to the Moon but hardly bothered to go back, never mind on to our other neighbouring planets – *Discovery*'s journey to Jupiter's moon seems much further away today than it did in 1968. *2001* conveyed the sense that technology was an integral component of humanity's confident continuing development. Subsequent films that speculate about the Earth's future have generally dealt with technology as a causal element in our route to distopia – from *Mon Oncle* to *Exterminator* to *The Matrix*, technology as depicted in the cinema destroys the environment and takes away our freedom.

The cinema is a reflection, if somewhat distorted, of the real world – a world that is passing through a period of dramatic cultural, sociological and economic change. Some of this change results from innovations in specific areas such as communications, industrialisation, agriculture. Some is the result of dramatically altering attitudes to how we live our lives, our sense of global community, and our understanding of where human history has led us and what the future may hold. This can be seen most clearly in the opposing concepts of the future – either as something we create by contemporary activities and decisions or as an unknown country that cannot even be predicted, never mind influenced. It is becoming increasingly important that the artefacts we make to support our activities in the world, which are in many cases directly involved with human survival and progress, respond to these complex changes while also reinforcing a sense of continuity which aids stability and helps foster a mature functional society.

This agenda is not an easy one to address as the form of the manufactured object is also subject to violent change. Many of our most important artefacts are becoming smaller and more mobile while simultaneously becoming more powerful. Ten years ago nearly everyone went to a big metal and glass box fixed to the pavement to make a phone call; now they use a plastic-covered, battery-powered circuit board which they carry around in their pocket. Forty years ago a computer was the size of a room, twenty years ago the size of a television set. Now I can prepare this text on a plastic box the size and weight of a book. The laptop computer is such a flexible tool that my machine is also used by astronauts on the Space Shuttle to work out their trajectory and by scientists in the Atlantic to help count plankton numbers. The size of the smallest computers is now determined by human ergonomics (such as the width of the human finger) rather than by the technology that makes them work. The basis of design for such tools is the same as it is for buildings – the size of the human body and the activities that we carry out in conjunction with their use. Despite the dramatic operational changes that have taken place over the centuries, the physical essence of life has remained remarkably static.

The physiological requirements for human existence have stayed the same for millennia – and the rituals of living, though subject to alteration and variation, are universal and timeless. Human existence is regulated by the activities of life – work, leisure, rest. Though contemporary patterns of working and resting are dramatically different from those in the past, once beyond the primal human driving force of survival and security, the fundamental backdrop to these activities remains the same: labour being the pursuit of a goal such as the manufacture of a product or the organisation of an idea; leisure being the relief or exercise of the body and mind. Because of the much more diverse methods of achieving these objectives today, the variety of building types has become more numerous and the operational requirements that are demanded of these buildings more complex and more difficult to achieve. Architecture today must pass through a vast number of financial, contractual, planning, environmental and legislative barriers before it is realised. The contemporary construction situation is more complex than it has ever been and it is unlikely to become any simpler. In addition, once completed, modern buildings are now expected to be flexible, responsive, sustainable, intelligent – and, as always, they are also expected to represent our relationship with the world and express our cultural ambitions.

So, despite the continuity of human needs, does the complexity of the contemporary situation necessitate a profoundly different architectural process? Some would say yes. There have been many explorations of the potential of machine-based systems for providing the basis of a new architecture and lamentations of the fact that contemporary buildings do not respond to contemporary existence in the adaptable way that modern machines can. To give just one example, throughout the twentieth century it has frequently been asked, 'Why not make use of the technology of production line manufacturing strategies to make buildings?' Indeed, why not? Production line car manufacture has been around for eighty years, yet, despite a few flirtations with this potentially efficient construction process, the vision of the factory-built house has yet to be fully realised – the reasons for this may be associated with technological ability and economic reality. However, the reasons may also be linked to the intrinsic underlying purpose of architecture which demands it expresses a range of complex desires and ambitions, some of which are readily understood, some of which are virtually unquantifiable.

There are, however, some buildings that are clearly not only successful in continuing the difficult task of being social icons (and have been readily accepted by the public in this role) but also reflect the challenges and opportunities of newly emerged technologies. What qualities do they have which allow their users to be at ease with their form and character despite their physical representation of this confusing new age? Architecture, if it is an art at all, is a social art and its value can only be judged by the effects it has on people. People have obviously accepted many of the new opportunities of technology – indoor plumbing, central heating, international travel, computer games, satellite TV, Internet shopping! As long as they remain in control of the process and have the choice of whether to use it or not, it is accepted. Architecture is no different – it must be appropriate to purpose and responsive to need. Efficiency, immediacy, continuity and clarity of purpose are the attributes of successful buildings which are as recognisable now as they have been throughout human history. These are among the important cultural (and practical) reasons why old – some would say outdated – technologies persist. Most people who have a need to prepare documents now use computers, some still prefer a typewriter, some a pencil. Nomads travelling the plains of Asia 10,000 years ago would have used carbon fibre cloth in preference to animal skins if it had been available – but only if it had done the job for which it was intended at least as well as the material it replaced, and also only if there were no cultural or societal inhibitions to its use. Building is a cultural activity endorsed and made possible by social values and conventions and in many cases the innovative is neither desirable nor beneficial to this process. Like the pencil, traditional building methods will persist as long as human beings exist. Nevertheless, the opportunities afforded by new technology cannot and should not be ignored; new technology is the contemporary response to the way we live in the world, and has a profound influence on creating the economic and cultural setting for contemporary society. Perhaps it also has the potential to extend the basic standard of living benefits enjoyed in the developed parts of the world to many more of the Earth's inhabitants.

It is therefore the ambition of this book to explore how new technology can contribute to the design of architecture that is responsive to the practicalities of building in a changing world but also to the essential human need to create meaningful places. In order to do this I have selected a limited range of themes and I am aware the critical reader may think these are not the best, or most appropriate, and may indeed think of others. However, there are many paths through contemporary experience – to follow them all would result in an unwieldy, confusing, massive tome – an encyclopaedia of ideas, many in conflict. My ambition has therefore been to chart one path, though I hope it will be seen in the context of many others. This is nevertheless a difficult task and I am the first to admit that my struggle with this issue cannot be the definitive, nor the last word on this topic, but I hope it may at least be a contribution to the debate. Just as I was beginning to write, and was struggling with the archetypal doubts of the author ('No one will read it anyway' and 'Even if they do they are bound to disagree'), I met briefly and regarding another matter with the architectural writer and broadcaster Jonathan Glancey. We fell to talking about how the public discussion about architecture was so important, and then of why we both in our different ways write about it. Perhaps unsurprisingly we came to the same conclusion, that we write in order to try to understand. Setting down my thoughts on paper, working through them again and again, helps me understand better – not conclusively, but better. To those who read this book, my hope is that my thoughts help you to come to your own understanding.

Perhaps *2001* is not so disappointing after all – my twenty-first century viewing of Kubricks' film about the distant genesis of humanity, its imminent future and ultimate destiny has helped reinforce my conviction that our technological future is firmly founded in the past, perhaps more so in architecture than in any other field of applied design – and understanding the past and its continuum to this moment will undoubtedly help us to deal with the future.

PART 1

TECHNOLOGY, ARCHITECTURE AND MEANING

> '...the essence of technology is by no means anything technological'
>
> Martin Heidegger[1]

This book explores the way new technology influences the development of architectural form. It deals with the relationship between two areas of man-made activity that impact on contemporary life most profoundly: the application of science and the design of our environment. For the same reason that it is not necessary to understand the manufacture of a piano to appreciate the sound, this book is not a study of construction techniques – to explore the reasons why architecture takes the varied forms it does, and how these forms may change in the future, it is not necessary to explain how specific operations, materials and components work. However, to appreciate both music and architecture an understanding of intention and context does help, therefore the focus of this exploration is the meaning and value of architecture in relation to human-made technology that shapes the world for habitation.

Technology is an all-embracing term that is used for an incalculable range of operations, objects, products, and events that constantly impact on all aspects of contemporary life. First coined by Harvard University professor Jacob Bigelow in 1828 as an all-encompassing word to describe general mechanical improvements it is now a term generally associated with the innovative, the new, the advanced – and leading on from that – the obscure; it frequently identifies some object or process not capable of being fully understood by everyone. Prior to the Industrial Revolution, most people held the bewildering workings of a powerful nature in awe, yet the simple operation of almost everything man-made could be relatively easily comprehended. Today,

2 The Queen Mary in New York, photographed by A. Feininger in 1950.

virtually the reverse is true. Nature has been explained thoroughly and convincingly in a multitude of accessible television entertainments but the way in which the television signal is produced, transmitted, received and decoded is a mystery sitting in the corner of the living room. Technology cannot be understood by everyone therefore it is the province of the specialist, though paradoxically, practically everyone is now also a specialist of some type or another! We expect the owner of the television and video store to know how to program our set, the garage mechanic to reset the chip in our car's brain, the washing machine repairer to reprogram it when the water fails to heat up – it is very difficult to keep our most common machinery operational without expert assistance. And these are just a few ordinary domestic tools. Outside the home there is an escalating hierarchy of machinery that directly impacts our lives and over which we have no control: automatic bank tellers, aeroplanes, power stations – where do you stop? We generally understand sufficient to access the vast range of technology that surrounds us, but as to how it works . . . .

The documentation of technology is already available in countless books, manuals and textbooks that codify and explain the way things work and how they are supposed to be used. Often written by those who have created the technology – those who therefore presumably can explain it best, who consummately understand its function, though perhaps only within the specific sphere in which it operates, these documents are read by those who operate or use the technology – those few who are the specialists in that specific area. As technology becomes more omnipresent we all become specialists in at least one aspect of its use, and know a lot about our own field but very little or nothing at all about the rest. We are all specialists and non-specialists simultaneously, one foot in the pool of technological expertise, the other waving about in confusion. However, no matter how limited our personal involvement or understanding of its manifestation, everyone experiences the general impact of technology.

Though this book is primarily about how it affects the way architecture is made, technology affects every way in which we inhabit the world; as American historian David Nye has suggested, it is intimately connected with society at the most fundamental level for '. . . someone makes it, someone owns it, some oppose it, many use it, and all interpret it.'[2] There are good reasons, however, for using the design and creation of buildings for an explanation of technological impact. If we are trying to discover something about the essential truth of the way technology affects our lives then examining the area that helps establish the nature of our existence should be the object of our study. The human place in the world is defined by a wide range of complex relationships, with people, with nature and, of course, though less easy to name, with our sense of personal existence – which might be called our spirituality. Another essential and important part of how people establish their existence is in relation to 'things' – objects without life. This is not as materialistic as it might at first sound: the thing might be an old photograph, a precious gift, an historic artefact. Part of this world of things that surround us is our buildings – not just the house in which we live, but all the buildings we use. The philosopher Martin Heidegger believed that the most important part of 'being' that defined our existence was to dwell – to be beneath the sky, on the Earth, in relation to other mortals and the divinities. He stated that 'being' happens in the place which discloses our existence, our identity, and this occurs most powerfully when we dwell, and 'we attain to dwelling, so it seems, only by means of building'.[3]

Architecture is the most important way in which we change our environment. Though some other structures are individually of greater physical size, buildings exhibit the complexity of human ambition in a more meaningful way than a road, a bridge or a wall. Also, when grouped together, buildings make cities which are perhaps the ultimate human-made creation. The main challenge to this achievement might eventually prove to be pollution, the ultimate effects of which have yet to be independently determined. That architecture is such a rich expression of our aspirations and ambitions is remarkable and fascinating; Giedion called it the 'unmistakable index to what was really going on' in any period of history.[4] The words of John Ruskin, perhaps the most significant nineteenth-century commentator on human shaping of the built environment, still ring true:

> *A picture or poem is often little more than a feeble utterance of man's admiration of something out of himself; but architecture approaches more to a creation of his own, born of his necessities, and expressive of his nature. It is also, in some sort, the work of the whole race, while the picture or statue the work of one only, in most cases more highly gifted than his fellows. And therefore we may expect that the first two elements of good architecture should be expressive of some great truths commonly belonging to the whole race, and necessary to be understood or felt by them in all their work that they do under the sun.*[5]

Buildings are powerful barometers of almost every aspect of human achievement, capable of expressing ideas about society, culture, religion, government, education, economics and, of course, technology. People can and often do love or hate the built environment that has been created for them or by them. They adopt buildings with which they had nothing to do in conception, design or realisation as their own and go to great lengths to protect their existence. Alternatively they can bring massive effort to lobby for the total destruction of whole areas that were built with good intentions for their benefit. In many cases there are clear, understandable reasons for either loving or spurning these buildings but sometimes people form attachments to ugly, impractical places too. Places are conglomerations of people, organisations, memories, as well as buildings, though it is the buildings that seem to represent all these elements most. Buildings – though just things – become an embodiment of what it means to dwell in that place, of a collective achievement. People love a city for its beauty, its vitality but they also continue to love it when it is dirty, polluted and crime-ridden. This is not an infatuation – it is a tried and tested love affair where there are disagreements, spats and arguments but love is deep and appears to persist 'warts and all'. When people object to a building project or seek to have a building removed, it is not that they believe that we should stop building forever; rather, what is in contention is how or what or where we build – the fact that we do build is never in question. This is more than just an acknowledgement that buildings are necessary for us to carry on our working, resting and leisure activities; it is an affirmation that building is an essential component in our understanding of existing in the world and, perhaps more important, of human advancement.[6]

We *must* build in order to establish our place in the world and, as in anything we do, technological innovation is an essential part of that process. Heidegger believed that advancing technology is a part of our human destiny and if one is to talk about the essence of existence, technology is a component of that essence. 'Technology is a means to an end … . Technology is a human activity. The two definitions of technology belong together … a man-made means to an end established by man.'[7] This statement helps define what technology is in a general sense and also clarifies how we understand technology. It also takes us back to the idea suggested at the beginning of this chapter; you have to be a specialist to understand how a specific technology works, but the underlying meaning of its impact is capable of being understood by everyone.

CONTROLLING TECHNOLOGY

Everything made by human beings is technology, consequently, it engages with every physical activity we undertake. The technician is someone who deals with the machine, with its efficiency and operational parameters rather than with meaning and truth. However, if technology is so all pervading and also at the core of defining our existence, perhaps the definition of the technician's role is too restrictive. The root of the Greek word *techne* means the activities and skills of the craftsman, and this aspect has been recognised in relation to building perhaps most cogently by the architect Renzo Piano. He perceives it as the architect's duty to comprehend materi-

3 Collision of the Cosmos *and the* Busley *at a balloon race in Brussels in 1909.*

ality and to use this skill to manipulate form in order to make beautiful and useful space: 'In my way of working, I never start a project merely on the basis of just a philosophy. Right from the first moment I think about materials, modes, *techné*, about which process to adopt and the right materials for it.'[8] But *techné* also refers to the abilities of the artist and most would acknowledge that it is the artist and not the technician who has done most to reveal the essential aspects of what it is to be human. That the two are reconciled, at least in the root of the word, is a boost to the effort to establish the meaning of technology in shaping the world today. If technology does emerge from both our practical 'making' side and our 'artistic' thinking side, this reinforces Heidegger's contention that technology is an integral part of our destiny.

Though technological advancement is apparently inevitable it does not follow that we automatically know how to apply it wisely as it emerges. In recent times, debate has focused more and more on whether or not we should use new techniques that have become available. Worldwide concern and debate about the use of such developments as weapons of mass destruction, organ transplants, cloning and genetically modified foods are contemporary and on-going. However, the word technology is often also used as an endorsement to attach value and relevance to products – what would a new car be worth if it did not incorporate 'the latest technology'?[9] Paradoxically, excluding technology from an area of human activity also adds value, suggesting an honesty and clarity that was not there before – one example is the increase in the marketability of 'organic' food. This sort of debate is not new; a hundred years ago similar arguments took place about factory production, the introduction of the motorcar and contraception. Concern about technological advance is sometimes identified as a moral issue; however, it is more directly linked to uncertainty about the future, fear of the unknown and of powerful forces out of control. This fear is not of the technology itself but of how it might be used. Proponents of the case for the nuclear deterrent now smugly make reference to a world without a major international conflict in more than fifty years – but has the technology ever been in the hands of those who might really use it? The worldwide uprising against nuclear weapons has now largely subsided, not because the threat no longer exists but because we have put it out of our minds, we have desensitised our fears on this issue. Otherwise, how can one rationalise the current concern about some future, as yet unidentified, illness that might result from corn that has been genetically modified to grow faster and larger, and by comparison equate it with our earlier terror at the prospect of the mass destruction of whole cities in less than five minutes by intercontinental ballistic missiles? The threat of technology is that it so obviously puts us in a position where we clearly cannot control it.[10] The control of technology in this sense is therefore a societal issue. An open society leads to public debate, political pressure and, slow though they may seem in coming, changes. Pressure groups like the Campaign for Nuclear Disarmament played an essential role in monitoring the excesses of government with regard to the deployment of nuclear weapons. Similar groups with other agendas have an important role in motivating public opinion on the way other technologies (for example, genetic modification) are implemented.

With his customary directness, Adolf Loos stated: 'There is no point in inventing anything unless it is an improvement.'[11] Assuming innovative technology can be controlled, how is it possible to use it to improve the world by improving what we build? New technology is generally employed in two ways: first, and perhaps most commonly, to improve an existing method or system; second, to make possible a new technique. The route from the discovery of a new scientific principle and its application is not generally straightforward; frequently a new technology developed for one role is transferred into other roles, sometimes far more useful and far more common than the first. An incredibly costly development exercise can be justified on the grounds of the value that the resultant spinoffs will have in less glamorous areas of human activity; for example the 1960s' space programme resulted in new applications as diverse as liquid quartz crystal displays and weather satellites. The same holds true for military research which has an enormous worldwide budget. Relatively few individuals would support research that is only there to support armed conflict; however, there is no doubt that much military innovation eventually finds practical peacetime applications. During the two world wars technological advance escalated dramatically with many quantifiable developments that have provided lasting benefit. Radar, telecommunications, computing, the jet engine, medicine – all made enormous advances during the Second World War.

The added value of spinoffs is incredibly important to general technological advancement because, surprisingly, comparatively few industries have dedicated research and development agendas commensurate with either their needs or the potential benefits which might accrue. The nature of the building industry in the UK – a number of large general building contractors and specialist house builders and a myriad of smaller firms all supplied by thousands of independent component manufacturers – does not lend itself to coordinated research. Government-sponsored research in universities and other specialist institutions is relatively limited compared to the industry's expenditure. When one compares the impact on our lives, there is much in common between the building industry and other industries that do maintain research and development as a large part of their budget. Big drug companies need research and development to create the range of new brand drugs they register each year. Software designers constantly create new products and update existing programs to maintain their market share. By contrast it could be convincingly argued that while these hi-tech industries are actively engaged in envisioning what the future may hold for us all, the future of the built environment is left to chance. With a few exceptions new technology in the building industry has largely resulted from spinoffs and its application is the result of determined work by a relatively small number of architects, engineers and designers who are concerned with making the most of what we have today as well as speculating on what tomorrow's architecture will be like. At present, the introduction of technological innovation is random and uncoordinated and consequently it is not tuned to what the industry needs. In the short term, this makes it even more important that we use what is available as best we can. For the future, it is important that long-term technological research should become part of a programme of quantified desires and responses determined by clients and users.

If we are trying to find out how technological innovation can best be used to improve *what* we build, it is important to recognise that this is not necessarily the same as asking the way to improve *how* we build. Efficiency and economy in building methods do not automatically lead to better buildings. The first of the Royal Institute of British Architects Future Studies papers, *The Value of Architecture*, explores the nature of quality in architecture and how it can be measured but concludes:

> ... the value of good design in architecture remains an elusive concept. The techniques for capturing economic value within the context of market forces are well represented and skilful, we are adept at exchange value but have still to weld to this technique the means of measuring the benefits that well designed buildings bring to the social, political, urban, and image values.[12]

One field of architecture where improvements would be especially beneficial is housing – however, until recently, the task of solving the housing shortage in the UK was seen by both local and national government as the provision of space, determined by objective standards and with adequate servicing, for as many families as possible within the budget. Public relations stressed the provision of bathrooms and central heating but the bottom line was the number of families that had been housed. Economical building was perceived as the main issue. New technology provided the ability to build repetitive apartment blocks, often high-rise, and though such buildings, if well designed, can work in certain situations, this solution has proven unsuitable for many places and cultures. Cheap low-rise housing with little investment in infrastructure and amenities has also failed to meet the inhabitants' needs. The common factor in failed community housing projects is a lack of attention to what is deliv-

4 Mass housing in Budapest – though buildings of this type can be found in any major conurbation in the developed world.

ered in quality in preference to quantity. Technology may make it possible to build more efficiently and more economically but the benefit of this should be to provide more good quality buildings with the same resources, rather than the same number for less cost. Technology should therefore be seen as a prime component in improving quality rather than reducing cost.[13]

The problem of social housing provision reinforces the complexities of bringing design innovations to bear on the problems that need solutions. Undeniably there is a shortage of quality housing for some groups in the UK – for these people inadequate housing is leading to health and social problems and for some, particularly the young, dedicated suitable provision is sometimes not available at all. This is clearly unacceptable. In the UK, a new housing policy targeting the needs of those in the most inadequate accommodation first, putting all resources into that area before building any more top-end luxury houses, would seem an achievable if unlikely solution. If we compare the problems in the UK with the housing shortage in India where a good proportion of the urban population lives in cardboard shelters or worse, British domestic problems seem trivial. To bring development techniques familiar in the West to bear on the Indian problem would be reasonable and beneficial. One can imagine sensitive local designers working with people's representatives, identifying urban sites, seeking out new industries that require a labour force, planning communities filled with schools, parks and houses tuned to the people's desires and way of life. Despite the varying degree of the problem, in both these situations the impediments to a solution are identical. Achieving the political impetus to deal with the problem is much, much more important than any technical or constructional issue. Without the overriding will of society such objectives cannot be realised.

Though an immediate solution to these examples is unlikely to appear overnight, this does not mean that the impact of new technology has no part to play in improving housing provision. In certain situations, political inertia can be overcome by showing how technical problems can be realistically solved and, when the situation arises, how effective projects are built because there is a ready and appropriate response at the right time. For example, the fire that followed the Hanshin-Awaji earthquake in the urban area of Kobi, Japan, was particularly devastating in some neighbourhoods because the already inadequate water supplies and difficult vehicle access were exacerbated by the earthquake disruption and caused insurmountable problems for the emergency services. Subsequently, the opportunity was taken to redesign these urban areas based around existing community groups but with new wider roads, updated services and social and commercial amenities. New building techniques were adopted to rebuild speedily large numbers of new dwellings that not only improved living standards and maintained individuality, but did so in a building form that provided security from further similar disasters. In North America, commercial manufacturers have developed the factory-made mobile home, and by assiduous government lobbying have been able to alter prejudicial legislation to make a much cheaper form of good quality housing available to millions of low-income families. Even in the UK quality design and innovative manufacturing techniques sponsored by

5 Elevated highway and surrounding residential property destroyed by the Hanshin-Awaji earthquake, Kobi, Japan, 17 January 1995.

6 A factory-made house built in Kobi to replace a dwelling lost in the earthquake and fire. The client designed their own building in a sales room on a computer with the aid of a sales assistant. The house components were prefabricated and delivered to site for assembly by the factory specialists in under six weeks.

1.1 Exterior

1.2 Exterior detail

Case Study

The Peabody Trust, Murray Grove Housing, Hackney, London, UK

Cartwright Pickard Architects' prefabricated housing project for the Peabody Trust housing association (which previously primarily undertook refurbishment projects) was selected in the Housing Design Awards 2000 for their forward looking solution to a common problem. The designers worked with Yorkon, a subsidiary of the UK market leader in temporary buildings manufacture Portakabin, to develop and prototype a modular volumetric steel housing unit that could be factory made complete with all plumbing, electrics, doors, windows, bathroom and kitchen fittings, tiles and carpets, and delivered to site for speedy assembly. The main contractors were the British building arm of the Japanese company Kajima, selected for their experience of factory made component assembly work. As well as the main dwelling units, prefabricated modules were used for the stair tower and lift, and the roof and balconies were assembled on site from factory made part-assembled steel components. Clip on terracotta cladding panels form the external wall layer. Site construction time for a project of this size was considerably reduced to under six months and though the cost was 15% more than the norm for similar housing, the project is perceived as a development prototype which will be studied over the next three years. If it is successful in technical and resident response terms then cost savings for future projects should be significant. This is a real project, inhabited by the Trust's usual clients, and it is important that it is they who will have a large say in the future development of this sort of housing. The Peabody Trust is also developing an environmentally friendly housing/workplace project on an urban brown field site with architect Bill Dunster and environmental specialists BioRegional that will be the first large-scale UK housing project that is 'carbon dioxide neutral', i.e.: it does not to add to the amount of carbon dioxide in the atmosphere.

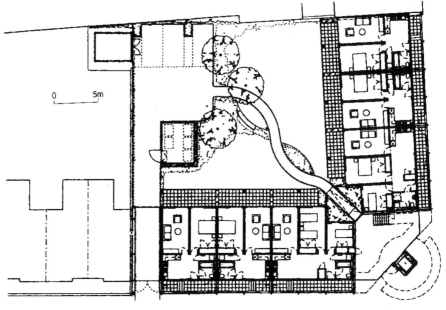

1.6 Ground floor plan

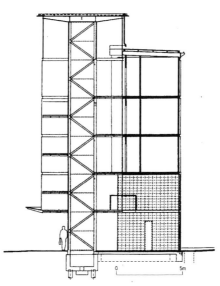

1.3, 1.4 and 1.5 Construction assembly

1.7 Section through stair tower

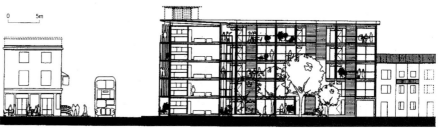

1.8 Site section

housing associations such as the Peabody Trust have led to the introduction of a high-density, low rent, urban housing close to sources of employment.[14] Designers and manufacturers may not always have the political influence to make improvements happen but they are absolutely essential in providing the physical means. Another factor present in the success of these three different solutions is their response to specifically regional problems. Despite the global implications of technological innovation, regionalism is still an overriding factor in the design and manufacture of buildings and the built environment. In an increasingly international economy where all developing nations aspire to the architectural symbols defined by the West as signifying commercial power it may be overlooked that factors associated with climate, topography, culture, society and economy are still core elements in the design of appropriate architecture.

So, while efficiency and economy are important, the ultimate aim of innovative design is to find out how to make more appropriate, more beautiful, more efficient buildings for more people. Can the application of innovative technology do this? It can be argued that the most appropriate buildings should not challenge their users' preconceptions and that within the traditional forms of architecture building solutions can be found to support all our needs. It has been argued, too, that in the field of architecture the best technology is that which is consummately familiar to those who use it. Traditional architecture (by which the exponents of this view means everything from the half-timbered cottage to high Classicism) is the solid foundation upon which to base a changing world. The counter argument is that there are no alternatives here – in a world of global trade, incipient conflict and dwindling resources, information technology and energy efficiencies have become more and more important in our lives and we have fully to embrace these new assets in order to survive, never mind improve our quality of life. A diverse, ambiguous, adaptive, responsive, technologically conceived architecture is an essential reflection of global change.

Despite these polarised philosophies it is important to recognise the unifying basis of architectural form. Everything that is man-made, from thatched roofs to Teflon coated membranes, can be categorised as technological – there are only degrees of familiarity. Why are some technologies as acceptable as if they had emerged straight from nature? Why are some threatening? The reason is that people make up their minds based on their personal response to the world as they see it. In order to progress this investigation further it is therefore necessary to explore the basis of the complex relationship that all of us have with architecture and the human-made environment.

THE ROLE OF CONTEMPORARY ARCHITECTURE

What does architecture do? The obvious response to this question is that it supports, protects and nurtures our activities at work, rest and leisure. The influential architectural historian Nikolaus Pevsner maintained that there is a difference between architecture and 'mere building' – how can a cathedral be categorised in the same way as a garden shed?¹⁵ Certainly, some buildings are destined to be the setting for the more public occasions in life, but momentous events can happen anywhere, even in a garden shed! Though the vast majority of building carried out in the world is not designed by architects that does not exclude it from being understood within the parameters of the term 'architecture'. Most now agree that Pevsner's desire to denigrate a particular form of building as not worthy of being included in this description is not only unrealistic but dangerous. For with the recognition that all building has an impact on the architectural world comes the responsibility to make it as good as it can be – if it is only to be a garden shed then make it one that fulfils its practical purpose well, contributing positively to its setting in any way it can. In this way we can and have achieved beautiful sheds, stimulating multistorey car parks, and exciting tunnel ventilator shafts… and more.

The absence of architects is not a problem either – some of the best and most forward looking architecture has had nothing to do with architects. Who would argue that some of the most beautiful, appropriate, ecologically aware buildings in existence in the world today are those that have been made by indigenous people using skills and techniques developed within their community by generations of practical experience? Such buildings, made from local materials, finely tuned to local climates and conditions, seem to have a oneness with their place that is recognisable to all, including those without specialist architectural knowledge. It is only in the twentieth century that vernacular architecture generally came to be viewed in this light. The turning point was perhaps the exhibition *Architecture Without Architects* at New York's Museum of

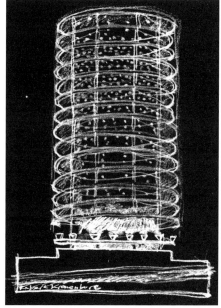

7 Toyo Ito, Tower of Winds, 1986. Water tank and ventilating tower with 1,300 lights that are operated by the shifting direction and strength of the wind – even the prosaic has potential to be poetic.

8 Toyo Ito, Egg of Winds, 1989. Moving images projected onto the city street.

9 Trulli *in Southern Apulia, Italy – a building type that has changed little over 2000 years.*

Modern Art in 1964 and curated by Bernard Rudofsky (his book of the same name has been continuously in print since that date). The formally trained architect has special reason to wonder at the beauty of such buildings.[16] This architecture has been built by people who understand implicitly the environment in which they work and have a code of rules to follow to ensure success within their limited pattern of forms and methods. Grouping of such buildings also results in a remarkable homogeneity in settlement form without formal planning or zoning guide lines. These buildings and groups of buildings form an undiluted expression of their inhabitants' place in the world – as direct as it can be because they have a significant continuing personal investment in the place. And though these simple buildings also have practical roles that nurture day-to-day activities and rituals, this role of identifying the inhabitants' presence in the world is readily recognised as a very important function.

In the developed world contemporary buildings made by architects, engineers, builders and manufacturers also have practical roles to nurture living and working activities. However, the opportunity for the users' personal involvement in the building process has been limited by a society that depends on specialists to negotiate the

10 *Occupying space, a temporary cafe beneath the Info-Box in Potsdammer Platz, Berlin.*

more complex technical, commercial and legislative boundaries of its building system. The individual has limited opportunities to build for him- or herself.[17] Does this mean that the role fulfilled by architecture of establishing the place in which one dwells is distilled? Or even lost completely? The answer is no. People identify with the houses that have been built for them, which they have adapted to their own use in countless ways and which have become a setting for their actions and their memories (the current DIY boom is merely a formalised expression of what has always occurred in a less commercially exploited manner, by storing possessions and arranging furniture and pictures). People also have a complex relationship with their neighbourhood – the church, the school, the shop – and with their city. In a different way, the most impressive buildings of a city become the landmarks for local and outsider, for those who know the place well and for people who have never even been there. Age or function of the building seems to be immaterial – though the fact that a building has a civic or public function is of course relevant as it more easily becomes part of the individual's own history. In the thirteenth century the cathedral of Notre Dame was undoubtedly a significant presence in the mind of the Parisian, in the seventeenth century the Palace of the Louvre was added to his mental map (though it did not become a public building until the nineteenth century), in the nineteenth century the Eiffel Tower, in the twentieth the Beaubourg Centre. To be a Parisian is to identify with these buildings as part of your sense of who you are. To the visitor they are the landmarks that confirm that you really are in the place you wish to visit. All these buildings have uses, they are servants/tools, but their most significant role for people is as immutable icons that signify both a sense of place and the identity of the individual. Such buildings identify the places that allow people to exist.[18]

The essential role of architecture as the manifestation of a person's presence in the world has, however, in some cases been confused with its other more pragmatic task as a tool. That architecture does have a real and valuable use is important in that it enables the individual to interact with it in a way they can never do with a work of art (to which their response must, of necessity, be primarily voyeuristic). However, when all other criteria are excluded from the design of a building except for its usefulness, and it is treated merely as an expedient means to an end then problems may arise with its role in establishing place and identity. It is such expediency which has led to the international confusion of architectural styles and the proliferation of non-geographically rooted building, the 'no-place'.[19] In order to explore this issue we first need to identify the 'no-place' clearly, though virtually everyone in the developed world will have been there. It is a landscape, generally urban, which has no significant identifiable features, which could be anywhere, in any nation, on any continent, in any climate. Its locale is defined by multinational commercial organisations, it has simplistic access patterns generally created solely for the car, any preexisting topographical pattern has been excised. The building forms are either anonymous or overtly referential to some archetypal clichéd pattern that has found its inspiration in any place other than this. A major misunderstanding about the proliferation of 'no-place' is that it is the buildings created without care and thought that are its prime instigator. Such development is hardly likely to lead to meaningful places, but isolated bad buildings have always existed and always will, and they are easy to replace as fashions and development trends change. 'No-place' architecture is more sinister than mere carelessness, 'no-place' architecture is designed to be that way – it is the result of a carefully determined strategy to bring all the economic factors of business down to the lowest common denominator; architecture is just the most visible sign of this policy. It may be described as efficiency, however, it is actually *ruthless* efficiency that leaves little space for human individuality. Its success is founded on the human desire for safety and familiarity, placing individuals in the situation where they must choose between what they know will be at least adequate in terms of service and quality, and the possibilities of something much more real, more intense, but also – perhaps – different and challenging. 'No-place' architecture is a result of the multinational strategy to remove the impediments to commerce that derive from differences in language, society and culture. 'No-place' architecture is at once comforting and frightening. It provides something that on the surface is familiar but in reality has no substance. It negates the need to travel because you are already there, but *there* is no-where.

One could be confused into believing that 'no-place' architecture results from the trend towards global commerce and internationalism. However, a world linked by international businesses, organisations and agreements is not in itself the problem – this is an inevitable trend that has its roots in the need for communications which has literally always been a part of human society. Thor Heyerdahl's epic voyages in *Kon-Tiki* (1947) and *Ra* (1969) were practical experiments that sought to establish the theory that despite the great distances involved, international communications and trade took place in prehistoric times – he set out to prove what was already clearly apparent from cultural similarities.[20] The contention was that the cross-fertilisation of societies is something that has developed the richness of world cultures. The twentieth century saw a massive acceleration of this process which has always taken place, physically through improved rail, road and sea transportation and the spread of air travel, but more significantly through telecommunications. Similar to technological advance, and partly dependent on it, intensified internationalism is also our destiny.

In the twentieth century, instantaneous free communication anywhere in the world via the Internet signals the emergence of a new global community. Will this stop people wanting to travel? This is unlikely according to the airlines who are currently ordering from Airbus Industrie the A380, the latest generation of large capacity passenger aircraft which will be able to seat up to 850 people on non-stop long-haul flights up to 14,000 km.[21] The availability of easy physical communications and trade is an essential element of global economy and interdependence, providing mutual responsibility and, it is to be hoped, understanding.

The Gaia phenomenon (whereby people are now beginning to identify not only with their locality, their nation, but also with their world) is a result of this international awareness. The idea of the Earth as a biosphere – a self-regulating sensitive organism whose existence depends on a symbiotic relationship between the planet and its

11 A380, the 850 seat long-haul airliner developed by Airbus Industrie.

life was developed by scientist James Lovelock in the 1960s – the name Gaia, from the Greek goddess of the Earth, was bestowed by his friend the author William Golding. Paradoxically, it is of interest that the essentially ecologically based success of this one world/one home concept has sprung directly from the manifestations of advanced technology such as easy international telecommunications and global television news, but perhaps most potently from the first clear images (made available in the 1960s from NASA's Gemini and Apollo programmes and the USSR's Vostock and Soyuz programmes) of the Earth relayed from space – our planet perceived more clearly than ever before as a finite place, beautiful and fragile.[22]

Despite the fact that it is advanced technology that has made it possible to identify our relationship with the world more clearly, it is the same application of scientifically based innovation that is widely perceived as the prime culprit behind the expansion of the anonymous environment: 'The technological backdrop is relentless. Worldwide electronic networks are transforming leisure and commerce, new digital markets are overlaying traditional trading patterns and routes. The pace of change, its fluidity and the sense of impermanence that new technologies engender can lead to a view that therefore design does not matter.'[23] An insensitive modern building set into an historic area is usually chastised for its modernity rather than its insensitivity. The technology whose by-product is more powerful weaponry, more catastrophic pollution, more faceless bureaucracy, is perceived as a sinister uncontrollable force without morals. But as we have already discovered, there are no evil machines. If there is evil, it is in how the technology is used – the dilemma is how to ensure it is used well and with sensitivity.

12 The Earth photographed from Apollo 17 *in 1972.*

Usually with every advance there comes change, and change usually implies upset and controversy. Defence of the status quo is an understandable aspect of human nature. It is also not without value as a conservative input into change helps ensure that proper consideration is taken before it is allowed to take effect. One solution to the dilemma of modern building, and one which has been repeatedly revisited, is to return to easily identifiable, pre-modern technology, architectural forms. Planning control in the UK in the second half of the twentieth century has been primarily based on this philosophy – encouraging similarity in materials, in form, and in 'style' to that historically found in a particular locale regardless of the function of the building or its internal requirements. We therefore have the paradox of buildings made with completely modern structural systems, environmental control and communications equipment that are dressed up to look – on the surface only – like something from the past. This is exactly what 'no-place' architecture needs to flourish – the freedom to place homogeneous functions within a reassuringly inoffensive but meaningless facade.

Another option is to be honest about the techniques and materials of the past and use them to the best of our ability and knowledge today. Keeping crafts and techniques from the past alive is important if only to ensure that the skills are available to repair important buildings from these periods. But what about making new buildings using these old skills? Though traditional building techniques have much to teach the contemporary architect and are appropriate in some situations, it is hard to imagine how such buildings could meet all the demands of modern life.[24] In some ways new technology is making a simpler, more sustainable existence possible for the individual, by allowing complex remote working scenarios where people can do business without having to travel to meet face to face. However, there are challenges which buildings in the twenty-first century must meet that cannot be achieved through traditional techniques – hyper efficient use of energy, use of renewable resources, safety from fire and natural disaster, higher levels of protection for sensitive equipment, and of course the preservation of the individual's identity. Identity is not the same as it was in the twentieth century or the nineteenth or any earlier age. Our recognition of place is made up from those buildings which come from earlier periods but our sense of ourselves stems from the era in which we exist today. New buildings are the symbol of a developing vibrant society. If we build in the style and manner of an earlier society what does that say about us. Respectful? Yes. Valuing our heritage? Yes. But forward-looking? No. If the role of architecture is to be both as a tool and a symbol then it must construct the future as well as preserve the past, it must symbolise our aspirations as well as our recollections. 'No-place' architecture cannot do this because it is just a tool that has lost its underlying purpose – that purpose, to provide its user with the awareness of who and what he is, is a fundamental role of architecture.

THE TECHNOLOGICAL CHARACTERISTICS OF ARCHITECTURAL FORM

The relationship that technology has with architecture is complex and confusing. We have discovered that the fundamental role of architecture is directly connected with human beings' sense of who and what they are; this then leads us on to the question, what part of human creativity is primarily concerned with the fulfilment of this purpose? Are we problem solving when we make architecture? Or are we expressing an aesthetic sense aimed at fulfilling some less easy to codify need? This question of how we understand architecture is directly connected to an old conundrum, is architecture an art or a science? Or, for that matter, a craft or an industry? The history of the profession of architectural design is run through with this question. The earliest buildings in every part of the world were created by people who both made and used them – in this scenario everyone was a builder. As cultures developed and larger structures such as shared dwellings or community buildings were required, one person or group of persons generally took control of the work, massing the workforce and materials together to make a coherent working group. In some cultures where other important artefacts, such as boats, could only be made by group activity, the building strategy was very similar. Where building construction became more complicated, perhaps in response to more difficult environmental conditions or where a social group was able to make a surplus (for example in agriculture) expertise could be brought in and specialists emerge, either in manufacture or assembly. Examples of continuing vibrant vernacular architectural form still exist in many parts of the world where cultural change has occurred with less urgency. Vernacular architecture, far

13 A central Asian yurt, the Kygyz *boz uy*, Kyrgzstan.

from being crude, is sophisticated and responsive to people's needs, environmental conditions and available materials and techniques. Indeed, it makes use of all the technology available in order to maximise its operational potential. One example may be found in Central Asia where the traditional dwelling for nomadic people is the yurt or *ger*, an archetypal manufactured building, its design standardised for millennia, variations brought about by individual manufacturers, but tuned so well to its function that fundamental change has been unnecessary.[25]

This principle, though much more complex in layout and detail, of an industrialised process developed to manufacture a product that has been gradually improved through use and experience, was used in Classical times to build the buildings and cities of Greece and Rome. Principal components were frequently manufactured in remote locations and shipped large distances to their building sites. A developing system of building layout and design enabled new settlements to be established with clearly understood, proven planning principles integrating services (drainage, water supply, heating) and communications (roads, harbours, lighthouses) with domestic, commercial, industrial, leisure, and government facilities.[26] The architecture was designed to support the speedy introduction and stable presence of a powerful, operational autocracy. It is characteristic of the nature of these societies that despite the enduring and powerful image of this architecture, the designers and organisers of this work remain anonymous – politicians', warriors', philosophers' and poets' names have been passed down to us, but not those of the architects.

In the Middle Ages the master craftsman first emerges as a recognisable individual working within a guild of specialist colleagues who collectively valued and protected the skills they applied. In some cases in this period named craftsmen of buildings are known, but it is not until the Renaissance that an individual can finally be recognised as the author of specific buildings.[27] The age of humanism established architect/artists as learned individuals whose aesthetic and intellectual faculties were inextricably linked. Architectural pattern books based on Classical models gave detailed instructions regarding construction techniques in the same manner as artists' handbooks provided information on the creation and application of pigments, grounds and surfaces. The scientific complexity of both areas was comparable. However, despite the recognition that technical knowledge was an important part of making lasting work, the creative part of the process was seen as something quite separate from the tectonic. The expression of volume, space and light to pictorial effect was sustained by the ability to construct form, but the technology that enabled this did not, in general, provide the inspiration. The role of technology in architecture for the architect/artist was as an enabler.

Throughout the eighteenth and nineteenth centuries the massive advances in science and its applications affected all aspects of human development; however, the architectural profession was not prepared to meet the challenge. Most buildings were designed by a type of master mason who acted also as the main contractor.[28] For more prestigious buildings the architect/artist, trained in Beaux-Arts system, worked under the direct patronage from his client.[29] The task of this architect was clearly defined – enlisted to provide the buildings that the leaders of society deemed necessary, his duty was to search for an image, generally unconnected with the technical revolution that was taking place all around. This meant attention to 'style' – the appearance of a building rather than its substance. Though the work of the British Arts and Crafts designers was eventually hugely influential on the next generation of innovative designers across Europe, even this movement was based to a great degree on the rejection of machine-made objects in favour of individual craftsmanship. Paradoxically their appreciation of and involvement with the simplicity and honesty of materials led to a formal clarity which rather than being retrospective heralded a new beginning in applied design.[30]

This is not to say that technical innovation did not take place in building; it did, but it was not usually the concern of the architect. New materials, in particular cast iron and then steel, dramatically affected the way buildings could be made, but it was in the new factories, railway sheds, greenhouses, that these innovations were largely expressed, rather than in the polite formal buildings of the gentleman architect. It was engineers and manufacturers who grasped and exploited the possibilities of new technology using its capabilities to create new, ambitious architectural forms. Innovative construction techniques appeared first in the buildings that served the new

14 Contemporary illustration from the Illustrated London News of Joseph Paxton's Crystal Palace, London, 1851.

industry: cast-iron framed factories and warehouses, and metal portable buildings prefabricated sometimes thousands of miles away from where they would be erected to serve growing trade with the colonies. It was the more conspicuous buildings such as the Crystal Palace, London (1851), and the *Palais des Machines*, Paris (1889), fulfilling pragmatic needs that could be met in no other manner, that took the world by surprise.[31] These giant exposition structures were created by designers from outside the architectural establishment, inspired directly by the new materials and techniques that had become available and built to challenge the power and vitality of the steamship and the railway rather than the solidity and permanence of conventional building.

In the late nineteenth century individual architects emerged throughout the industrial world who began to struggle with the challenge that new materials and production methods brought. In hindsight it seems that these architects were struggling to catch up with the rest of the manufacturing industry – architecture was always at least a generation behind what was happening in the commercial world. This time-lag was at least partly due to the apprenticeship system in which designers must be articled to older practitioners in order to train for the profession. The Beaux Arts colleges that provided supplementary education remained attached to developing the lessons of antiquity – a knowledge of the 'styles' was the required passport to matriculation.[32] But new architectural forms that absorbed technology as an inspiration gradually emerged in Vienna with the *Secession*, in Germany with the *Deutsche Werkbund* and in Holland with *De Stijl*. The subsequent Modern Movement that changed the basis of architectural design was truly international, emerging with different cultural traits based on each geographical region.

15 Recycling the Crystal Palace? A contemporary proposal published in The Builder. *The builders, Fox, Henderson and Co, considered it would be possible safely to construct this 47-storey tower from the exhibition building's components.*

Eventually these different strands were brought together under a series of powerful manifestos that sought to grasp everything to do with the machine age as an opportunity for beneficial change. The momentous meeting during which the agenda for the Modern Movement was established took place under Le Corbusier's dominating influence in the Gothic chapel of the castle of La Sarraz near Lake Geneva in Switzerland in June 1928. Attended by most of the main protagonists from across Europe including Siegfried Giedeon who would later document the history of the movement, it was here that CIAM, the *Congrés Internationaux d'Architecture Moderne* was formed.[33] The turmoil of the First

16 Palais des Machines, *Ferdinand Dutert, 1889.*

17 De Stijl *architecture – Eigenhaard Housing, Amsterdam by Michel De Clerk, 1917.*

World War, the accelerated technological progress it brought, the massive cultural upheaval that ensued, and the devastated landscape could all be beneficial in creating a new built environment representative of the way people would live in the future. These ideas struck at the heart of architecture's role to express the way people inhabit the world and so rung true with those impatient with the past and anxious to build a better future.

In hindsight, what can be said of the Modern Movement buildings that are the legacy of this revolution? Reyner Banham stated that the International Style architects '… produced a Machine Age architecture only in the sense that its monuments were built in a Machine Age'.[34] In many ways Modern Movement architecture can also be seen as a genre of buildings that were the legacy of the nineteenth century rather than a precursor of the twenty-first. Its architecture represented an idealised, revolutionary view of the machine age, though in reality it relied primarily on appearance rather than technology for the creation of this image. Though there are many beautiful buildings that were built by Modern Movement architects, it can be argued that gifted individuals will produce wonderful objects in any style, and that Modernism was just that, a 'style' like that exhibited by the many Neoclassical and neo-Gothic buildings that were also erected at the same time.[35]

Unfortunately, an incontrovertible legacy of the Modern Movement was that in many of the large-scale projects created under its influence, the complex relationship between buildings, spaces and people that make up our cities was destroyed. A belief that the efficiency of factory production could be a model for the way we live led to the resulting mess of inhospitable, alien places, the worst of which were subsequently blown up and replaced in the 1970s and 1980s. This unsuccessful machine-age architecture resulted in an anti-modern backlash. In British house building every mock style from the past six hundred years was employed to create low-density estates that have in turn created long-term blight in Britain's cities and countryside, obscuring the boundaries between urban and rural and resulting in the virtual abandonment of the city centre for living. This is not a condemnation of all suburban living but of the absorption of green field sites by mass house builders because they are more profitable to build on, of the use of urban sites for low-density housing that does not recognise local building form, and of the rejection of city centres as places in which people can live as well as work.[36]

There was also a sustained attempt to reject the modern in large-scale buildings. The dissatisfaction with Modernism led to important realisations that more humble building could provide valuable insights into the way architecture fulfilled people's needs. Robert and Denise Venturis' convincing arguments presented in their influential books *Learning from Las Vegas* and *Complexity and Contradiction in Architecture* showed that the message of architecture sometimes emerged from simple clear analysis of the contemporary vernacular and that an honest language of easily understood architectural forms could be adopted for inexpensive building which would still have meaning and purpose. Their intention was to

> … reassess the role of symbolism in architecture, and, in the process, to learn a new receptivity to the tastes and values of other

people and a new modesty in our designs and in our perception of our role as architects in society. Architecture for the last quarter of our century should be socially less coercive and aesthetically more visual than the striving and bombastic buildings of our recent past.[37]

However, a misunderstanding of this message has led to the design of many buildings that have been inspired by a post-modern trawl through history for flippant motifs that can adorn 'functional' bland boxes, built in the most economical manner though equipped internally with the latest gadgets. As Tadao Ando states:

Postmodernism emerged in the recent past to denounce the poverty of modernism at a time when that movement was deteriorating ... postmodernist styles endeavoured to recover the formal richness that modernism appeared to have discarded ... Yet this movement, too, has quickly become mired in hackneyed expression, producing a flow of formalistic play that is only confusing rather than inspiring.[38]

18 *Post-modern Portland Building, Portland, Oregon by Michael Graves, 1980.*

Like the bland 'no-place' multinational approach to design, architecture that becomes a one-line joke is not sufficient to sustain the needs of its users, no matter how well-equipped it is inside. To maintain that there is a simple way to solve the complex issues of making contemporary meaningful architecture is to deny the seriousness of the problem.

Good architecture cannot result from separating out the different aspects of its character in order to create applied form. Architecture is an art, but it is integrated with craft, science and industry. It is all these things because it is an expression of all human activity. In times when people lived more simple lives, living close to the land or the sea, finding their own food, making all their own artefacts, architecture had a natural and direct link with their lives. The architectural forms were more simple though not necessarily unsophisticated in their approach to the issues of environment, climate, siting and function. These buildings used all the aspects of technology that were available to the buildings' makers. Today, the more complicated character of all aspects of life is reflected in the combined effort of the many skills that are necessary to create even the simplest building. To create something that still communicates the needs of the people who will use it while accommodating all the functional and environmental necessities is difficult; however, as in the past, it is still important to make use of all the available technology though the fact that there seems to be so much more of it to choose from makes this task much more complex.

HUMANISTIC ASSOCIATIONS WITH ARCHITECTURE

Architecture is an artefact, a thing, and yet because of its significance to human beings people frequently assign it human attributes. This also occurs with other manufactured objects, in particular machines which have a semblance of animation and autonomy; for example cars, ships and aircraft, and to a lesser degree anything that people operate. In very special circumstances the human relationship with a machine may become especially significant. Carolyn Grace owns and flies a wartime

Supermarine Spitfire Mk IX that her husband restored before his death:

> *Every time I see the Spitfire it thrills me, it's such a beautiful thing. When you climb up on the wing and slide the canopy open you get this wonderful, seasoned smell, a mixture of aviation fuel, hydraulic fluid and oiled metal. The cockpit is very narrow, and when you climb in, it sort of encases you within it. It's a very secure feeling. I've met many wartime pilots who describe that same feeling – of becoming one with the aeroplane.*[39]

Usually, though, when people have a relationship with a machine it is of a curiously dated kind. We believe that machines are a grade above our tools, that they are like servants, and it is hard not to believe a servant who prevents your tasks being completed is not doing this simply to thwart your ambitions – you become angry with it, distrustful, resentful. Similarly a reliable tool/servant is rewarded with loyalty and affection. People imprint their own personalities on to the relationship and identify good performance with cooperation, inadequate performance with poor behaviour. Though the relationship people have with architecture is related to this characteristic master/servant one there are significant differences.

The modernists maintained that a house was a machine for dwelling in – however, this core perception of the relationship between buildings and people was fundamentally wrong. It implies that we operate a house in much the same way as we operate an appliance. Take, for example, the washing machine, a device invented by the Shakers, a religious community based in North America. Their belief that heaven could be manifested in this existence on Earth led to a philosophy of creation and improvement of all the daily domestic artefacts associated with their rural life. As a group they strived to be independent and self-sufficient, making everything they used of the highest quality and efficiency, creating by this process a range of related products now admired for their ingenuity, simplicity, appropriateness and beauty. The range of products which they invented is prodigious, from clothes pins to sash weights, from the circular saw to condensed milk.[40] The washing machine was devised to remove the worst aspects of a largely unrewarding task in order to improve the life of the community. The modern automatic washing machine carries out this same task in a family setting. We learn how to operate the machine and use it when necessary. When unused it is dormant. If it gives reliable service we are pleased with it but at the back of our minds we know that some day it will break down and then it will need attention. If we want to use it but it is broken, we are frustrated and annoyed and resign ourselves to the extra cost of having it repaired or replaced – alternatively we go to the laundrette and rent someone else's machine. From this scenario it is easy to see that the human relationship with a washing machine is restricted to the basis of whether or not it is a good servant.

Our relationship with a house is different. A house is not operated, it is inhabited. There are activities related to operation, turning lights and taps on and off, opening

19 Shaker Laundry Room at Hancock Village, Massachusetts. The c.1820 washing machine is to the rear.

and shutting doors and windows, but we also clean it, paint it and furnish it. We make a fire, restock the fridge, water the plants – in other words we serve the house so it may fulfil our needs. These activities build up an understanding of the needs of the house and are similar to those we undertake for our children – feeding, dressing, bathing. In return we expect comfort and protection from inclement weather, from danger and from unwanted visitors. Also the house provides a refuge, the repository for our sleeping and waking life. We have an intimate servant/master relationship in which the roles are switched around depending on the activity.

This analogy of an alternating servant/master relationship operates for the other buildings associated with our lives. We may go to work in an office or a factory and we are the servants to the activity that takes place there, but these buildings also provide the venue for our friendships, the source of our income and they protect our activities from weather and danger as before. If we explore the various degrees of service that we require from a building this analogy continues to be applicable. When we go to a restaurant to eat, if it is just rest and sustenance, the decoration or ambience is not too important because we expect to pay primarily for the food. However, if the balance of servant/master is shifted one way or the other things begin to change. A more pleasant internal environment encourages people to linger and there are less meals served though they become more expensive. We enjoy the feeling of being served, of being comforted by the environment as much as the food. Alternatively, if sustenance is all we care about we buy take-out food and eat on the street, in our car, or back at our workplace which provides shelter for this activity too.

Surprisingly, the concept of the building being a machine for living in has been adopted most ruthlessly by the multinational companies that have attempted to reduce their restaurants, hotels and shops to a completely prescribed entity where entry into each of its outlets, no matter where it is in the world, is identical. In the case of a hamburger chain restaurant, you can go there and 'operate' the system quickly and efficiently with a commensurate reward in culinary satisfaction, but would you choose to eat there all the time? You can 'operate' a chain hotel room just as easily because you have been there before, but would you choose to live in one? You can stock up on basics in a chain supermarket, but is that the place to find a diverse range of local produce? This reinforces the idea that environments created on a mass-produced basis are not as much signs of increased efficiency as increased consumerism.[41]

If we accept that a house is not a machine for living, a factory or office not a machine for working, and so on, it makes it much easier to acknowledge our more deeprooted relationship with architecture. However, though we can now see that this assertion by the modernists was wrong, their fundamental desire to come to terms with the impact of technology on home and work – on life in general – was correct. Innovative technology is at the core of the increased complexity of contemporary life and this has changed the character of building types. To try to categorise architecture by purpose or style seems almost pointless today because there is such an intermingling of function and form. Instead of the more readily defined single roles of the past it is now common for new, large-scale, urban buildings to contain a mix of activities including dwelling, commerce, leisure and community space. Innovative technology has in the past resulted in new building types – in the twentieth century among others we saw cinemas, motels, garages and airports emerge. In the twenty-first we have some new building types such as telephone call centres, cyber-cafes and tele-hotels but perhaps more challenging is the removal of building types: conventional retail and travel services are set to change in the near future due to Internet sales.[42]

If the types of architectural function have changed, architectural form has become equally diverse. This is partly the result of the wide range of structural systems and material options available, but it is also due to an eclectic mix of design philosophies at work. This pandemonium of architecture is redolent of the age and though undoubtedly challenging, it is not necessarily something that leads to confusion in our understanding of what architecture means. It can be convincingly argued that each age has its architecture and this outpouring of ideas is commensurate with the emergence of a global civilisation. If Japanese cars are built in Sunderland and American computers made in Lothian, why cannot a British architect design the seat of the German Parliament and a Spanish architect design the seat of the Scottish Parliament.[43]

One way to explore our changing relationship with architecture is to examine the range of human characteristics that can be attributed to buildings, and it is also interesting to compare similar responses generated by buildings from the past with those of today, because this indicates the change that advancing technology has made. The nature of human feeling for architecture can be explored by examining just four responses, two generally negative, two generally positive, though there are undoubtedly other emotive responses which the individual might be able to attach to a building with which they have a particular personal involvement.

Negative associations are generated most strongly through fear, for example of aggression, and anonymity. A castle is an inherently aggressive piece of architecture yet beautiful in its simplicity. Its walls are austere, with carefully devised repetitive geometric forms. We understand its function and the purpose for which it was built, and perhaps its history also affects our response to its presence. We also appreciate that though this building was once a symbol of perhaps brutal oppression, it is now ridiculously ineffectual in its original role – technology has now rendered obsolete the purpose for which it was built. It is emasculated as a weapon of war, but as a building it retains substance and meaning. It is a physical message from the past – with a little imagination it is not too hard to visualise what it was like to defend those walls.

The aggressive Brutalist architecture of the 1960s seemed to reflect the powerful concrete forms of wartime bunkers, coastal defences and gun platforms. That such an architecture could emerge in the decades after the Second World War is understandable in terms of aesthetic inspiration but bizarre in human terms. Were the designers trying to do the architectural equivalent of poking flowers down gun barrels when they inhabited these forms with housing, schools, and hospitals?[44] Contemporary military force is sometimes secret (the ultimate indication of aggression is

20 Montealegre Castle, Vallodolid, Spain.

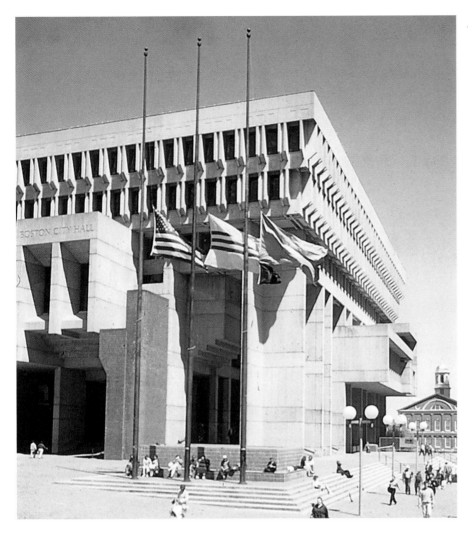

21 Castle, aircraft carrier and homage to Le Corbusier's monastery la Tourette – Boston City Hall by Kallman, McKinnell and Knowles, 1968.

22 Lockheed SR-71A Blackbird – *beautiful and menacing.*

the hidden weapon), but when visible it is mobile, volatile, and mechanistic – the warship, the tank, the Stealth bomber. It is the colour of camouflaged metal, and elements of its form are clearly not structural but there for other sinister, unidentifiable purposes. Architecture that uses this language uses technology as an expression of power. The Oscar-winning set design by Anton Furst for Tim Burton's 1989 *Batman* movie created a city of just such buildings to represent an autocratic empire but, in truth, no real commercial power would be foolish enough to state so clearly its intentions in its buildings. Architects fascinated with the power of these machines seem far more likely to transpose them into club interiors, shops, designer houses, even dental surgeries such as the Ark in Kyoto by the Japanese architect Shin Takamatsu described as a ' … monstrous, primitive, and mythical machine [which] ultimately does not disclose any previous function. It is an unknown mechanism, an unidentifiable object …' [45] Interestingly, *Batman*'s designer cites Shin Takamatsu among his influences.

Far more frightening than aggressive architecture is that which is completely

23 Dystopic design for Gotham's main street by Anton Furst for the 1989 film Batman.

24 Shin Takamatsu, The Ark, Kyoto, 1981–83.

anonymous, for the faceless facade can conceal anything. Anonymous architecture has found its best description in literature, in Franz Kafka's *The Trial* (1925) and *The Castle* (1926), where the societies which are described adopted a building style that mirrored the impenetrability of the social system. The fascist architecture of Albert Speer was designed to reduce the individual to a cog in the machine of society; vast simple forms, redolent of previous ages, but stripped down to emphasise scale and mass, to oppress the individual and deify the state. Stalinist architecture was simply big and repetitious. Although totalitarian states made use of the technical innovations in building construction that made it possible to erect huge, repetitive buildings at an acceptable financial cost, they were not the only bureaucracies in which such architecture flourished.[46] The housing programmes created to replace not only the stock of European buildings destroyed during the Second World War, but poor quality urban dwellings around the world, mistakenly prioritised speed and efficiency over care and consultation. Politicians, planners and architects believed that the provision of modern amenities and services was more important than individuality, and the flawed mass housing projects which provided people with a slot in a matrix rather than a place in the world were built.

25 Intimidating architecture – Grande Arche, La Défénce, Paris.

26 Albert Speer, New Reich Chancellery, Berlin, 1938–39. Stripped Classicism designed to emphasise the state over the individual.

27 'No-place' navigated though not identified by signboards.

28 Ernst Haeckel. A print from his 1904 book Kunstformen der Natur.

Contemporary commercial architecture is in many cases purposefully anonymous. Built to provide standard serviced space based on criteria set by the letting companies, the relationship between the organisations that act as clients by funding the building and those who use it is usually minimal. If a retail mall, the facade is there to play host to a range of brand names and logos; if for office or small business use, even this meagre source of identification is missing. In some cases even important sites in our cities are given over to anonymous architecture – a simplistic idea establishing the basis for the entire building form, but care in detail at the human level is missing. These can be and often are generic solutions that create no sense of place. Such buildings create instead snapshot architecture – a recognisable image from a distance that gives nothing to the people who use the buildings.

It is relatively easy to find positive human associations for buildings: welcoming, safe, friendly, grand, stimulating. However, building forms that have been shaped by the application of advanced technology that express complexity and mystery in their image are especially interesting. Though complexity can be confusing it can also be intriguing, and one can readily accept that, once understood, comprehension and knowledge will be the reward. The visual attendant to complexity is richness – in ideas, pattern or form. Nature is full of complex patterns and forms, and the belief that unravelling the meaning of these systems will bring knowledge is largely founded in experience. In architecture, visual complexity communicates investment in time and effort. In decorated architectural forms this may be all that is initially communicated; however, it generally fuels the belief that more careful investigation is worthwhile. Constructional or structural complexity communicates a more instant message. A trussed roof has many members working together in partnership, geometry and pattern, expressive of tension and compression. It is not necessary to understand the structural forces at work to appreciate the intention and the result. Advanced technology frequently makes use of complex pattern making to deliver its end result, woven fibres, circuit boards and computer chips being three examples at different sizes. It is amusing that writers seeking to prove the existence of technologically advanced visitors from other planets in the past have cited the detailed pattern making in Jain temples as an example of the influence such visitors might have left by suggesting the builders were copying circuit boards. This spurious suggestion at least underlines the fascination and beauty we associate with complexity.

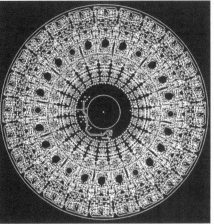

29 Integrated circuit design for a computer operated robot.

30 Jain temple ceiling (c. eleventh century).

Richard Rogers' Lloyds Building in London with its exuberant external detailing has been compared to the flying buttresses of a Gothic cathedral; Inmos, with its complex of masted, cabled elements sailing above the roof, to a harbour filled with square rigged ships. Bringing out the usually hidden elements of structure and servicing provides these buildings with an identity which is culturally familiar, though one that has perhaps not been associated with architecture before this. People make their own connections and identify with architecture in their own way – the expression of complexity gives them a conviction that effort has been expended to create something worth identifying with. Jean Baudrillard, the French sociologist, was clearly fascinated and maybe a little rattled by Richard Rogers' first major foray into this territory with partner Renzo Piano: 'Beaubourg-Effect … Beaubourg-Machine … Beaubourg-*Thing* – how can we name it? The puzzle of this carcass of signs and flux, of networks and circuits … the ultimate gesture towards translation of an unnameable structure …' but comes to some conclusion about what it all means: '… this *thing* openly declares that our age will no longer be one of duration, that our only temporal mode is that of the accelerated cycle and of recycling: the time of transistors and fluid flow.'[47]

Complexity may also promote feelings of fear, most probably emanating from incomprehension, fear of the unknown. Indeed, one attribute of some complex

31 Lloyds Building, London, Richard Rogers Partnership.

32 Inmos, Microprocessor factory, Newport, South Wales, Richard Rogers Partnership.

33 Beaubourg Centre, Paris, Renzo Piano and Richard Rogers.

modern buildings is that they are enigmatic, unsettled and indeterminate – an association which can best be described by a feeling of mystery. The mysterious is a familiar attribute of old buildings too. The earliest structures to which we have access, prehistoric monuments such as barrows and stone circles, are undoubtedly mysterious. This is because although we may know something about the site's function (for example that it is a burial site), we still have no clear idea of the rituals associated with these places, and sometimes the underlying purpose is in doubt. Clearly, our ancestors spent a vast amount of time and effort to create these places yet their role is now obscure.

34 Castlerigg stone circle, Cumbria, UK.

Another way in which these buildings are mysterious relates directly to the contemporary advances in technology that were necessary for their construction. We clearly have the physical object to examine in order to determine how the structures were made; but sometimes instead of providing answers this merely poses more questions. We can see how the stone was worked and how it was jointed, the formal intentions in creating space, but how were such large pieces erected? How were they brought to the site, sometimes over great distances? It is the ephemeral technology developed to create the permanent structure that is missing. Contemporary attempts to answer these questions have led to a new field of experimental archaeology that tests differing reconstructions often based on reinterpreting contemporary techniques to deduce their root source. We can now speculate with the benefit of some practical experience on the way in which the pyramids were built or the way the stones were transported for Stonehenge. However, the mystery remains – partly because in many cases the evidence is circumstantial and it may never be possible to come to a definite conclusion, and partly because increased knowledge of their techniques has engendered an increased wonder at the ancients' organisational and constructional skills.

Though we do not know for sure the purpose of many standing stones many believe they probably had some spiritual role, and if one looks for more recent buildings which also convey this quality we find they were usually also built specifically for this purpose. Religious buildings, even for those who profess not to believe, have a spiritual quality that is readily accessible by all. Perhaps it is the knowledge that the architecture expresses in the most physical way the faith of those who do believe. There is also something about the best of these buildings that manages to access a part of ourselves that we do not readily acknowledge in day to day life. A church, a mosque, a temple, a synagogue have all been created for a special purpose, a purpose associated with something we do not fully understand; there is a richness of history and cultural purpose behind these buildings that extends beyond self, family, community, nation … even beyond the world.

Mystery occurs not just in religion but in nature too. Though science is on a specific quest to understand the natural world there is a general underlying belief that we will never, no matter how long or how hard we try, understand everything. For many of us technology also has this effect; we feel we can see the wonder of it around us but we will never be able to understand it all. Almost everyone uses computers but how they actually work is a mystery. It is like alchemy, a process with scientific trappings that leads to inexplicable, magical results. The best contemporary architecture taps into this mysterious quality, using technology in wonderful subtle ways to mirror our relationship with nature – to quote Heidegger: 'to bring beauty to our relationship with the ground and the sky; to accept our movement through time and space'.[48] Complex, mysterious architecture can heighten our appreciation of the achievements of human creativity, illuminate the relationship it has with natural elements such as the landscape, plants and light, but still be clear about use and purpose. Such architecture gives us enough to help us realise who and where we are, but holds enough back so we can still wonder at the world.

35 Mysterious and beautiful, like a sailing ship moored on the Cambridge Fens – Schlumberger by Michael Hopkins.

Notes

1. 'The Question Concerning Technology' is the title of a lecture delivered by Heidegger in Bremen in1953 and published in Martin Heidegger, *Vorträge and Aufsätze*, Pfullingen: Günther Neske Verlag, 1954. This translation by William Lovitt is found in David Farrell Krell (ed.), *Martin Heidegger, Basic Writings*, Routledge, London, 1993 (first published 1978), p.311.
2. David E. Nye, *Electrifying America: Social Meanings of a New Technology 1880 – 1940*, MIT Press, Cambridge, Mass., 1990, p.ix.
3. Heidegger's lecture 'Building, Dwelling, Thinking' was delivered to the Darmstadt Symposium on Man and Space in 1951. This translation is by Albert Hofstadter and appears in David Krell (ed.), *Martin Heidegger, Basic Writings,* Routledge, London, 1993, p.347.
4. 'However much a period may try to disguise itself, its real nature will still show through in its architecture, whether this uses original forms of expression or attempts to copy bygone epochs …. It is an unmistakable index to what was really going on in a period …. architecture is indispensable when we are seeking to evaluate that period.' Siegfried Giedion, *Space, Time and Architecture: The Growth of a New Tradition*. Harvard University Press, Cambridge, Mass., 1967 (5th ed, repr. 1982), p.19–20.
5. John Ruskin, 'The Nature of Gothic' from *The Stones of Venice* (1853) in Lionel Trilling and Harold Bloom (eds), *Victorian Prose and Poetry*, Oxford University Press, London and New York, 1973, p.183.
6. Heidegger comments on this in 'Building, Dwelling, Thinking': 'However hard and bitter, however hampering and threatening the lack of houses remains, the *proper plight of dwelling* does not lie merely in a lack of houses ….The proper dwelling plight lies in this, that mortals ever search anew for the essence of dwelling, that they must *ever learn to dwell*.' David Krell (ed.), *Martin Heidegger, Basic Writings*, Routledge, London 1993, p.363.
7. Heidegger, 'The Question Concerning Technology', ibid. p.312.
8. Renzo Piano in Paul Goldberger, *Renzo Piano Building Workshop Buildings and Projects 1971–1989*, Rizzoli, New York, 1989, p.238.
9. The business section of *The Sunday Times* describes the design strategy behind the Jaguar X400 released in 2000: 'Not only will the craftsmanship and traditional Jaguar interior design be instantly recognisable, but executives have made great efforts to ensure the X400 has every bit of technological wizardry to match or beat the competition.' David Parsley, 'The Cat Prepares to Pounce', *The Sunday Times*, 8 October 2000, p.14.
10. Heidegger states: 'What is dangerous is not technology – technology is not demonic; but its essence is mysterious … . The threat to man does not come in the first instance from the potentially lethal machines and apparatus of technology. The actual threat has already afflicted man in his essence.' 'The Question Concerning Technology', in David Krell (ed.), *Martin Heidegger, Basic Writings*, Routledge, London 1993, p.333.
11. As quoted in Gevark Hartoonian, *Ontology of Construction: On Nihilism of Technology in Themes of Modern Architecture*, Harvard University Press, Cambridge, Mass., 1994, p.xiii.
12. Eric Loe, *The Value of Architecture: Context and Current Thinking*, RIBA Future Studies, London, 2000, p.52.
13. Dell Upton accurately describes the problem of mass housing as 'housing the non-consumer' as it consists of authorities providing for those who have little or no choice because they cannot afford to buy their way into an alternative. See Dell Upton, *Architecture in the United States*, Oxford History of Art, Oxford and New York, pp.239–43.
14. For more information on the Peabody Trust see their web site: *www.peabody.org.uk*.
15. Colin St John Wilson outlines the historical transition from the unity of architecture and building as understood by the Greeks via the application of the philosopher Kant's definition of Fine Art as essentially 'purposeless' to architecture, through Muthesias' 1902 distinction between 'Style-Architecture and Building-Art' to Pevsner's famous comparison. See Colin St John Wilson, *The Other Tradition of Modern Architecture: The Uncompleted Project*, Academy, London, 1995, p.61.
16. Bernard Rudofsky, *Architecture without Architects*, Albuquerque, 1987 (First published by Museum of Modern Art, New York, 1965). The first world survey of persisting vernacular building culture was published in 1997, edited by Paul Oliver, *The Encyclopaedia of Vernacular Architecture of the World*, Cambridge. The lessons that might be learnt from the manner in which vernacular architecture is designed and built are examined in Part III, under Intuitive Architecture.
17. However, where these opportunities have been taken up, either by self-build groups working within the system to recognise modern building patterns, or rogue individuals making highly personal eccentric homes with comparatively crude skills, they exhibit a passionate commitment to what they have acheived and an intimate connection with their dwelling. See part III, Alternative Architecture.

18 The building is a 'thing' made with technology but Heidegger also identifies it as the place where the 'truth of Being' happens; it is the place that reveals our existence. See David Farrell Krell's introduction to Heidegger's essay 'Building, Dwelling, Thinking' in David Krell, *Martin Heidegger, Basic Writings*, Routledge, London 1993, p.344.
19 Kenneth Frampton, in his essay 'Rappel á L'Ordre, The Case for the Tectonic' (1990) quotes Vittorio Gregotti: 'The worst enemy of modern architecture is the idea of space considered solely in terms of economic and technical exigencies indifferent to the idea of site...' See Kate Nesbitt (ed), *Theorizing a New Agenda for Architecture: An Anthology of Architectural Theory 1965–1995*, New York, 1996, p.524.
20 Heyerdahl's explorations were examples of experimental archaeology, in which he reconstructed ancient technology by building boats using traditional materials and methods and using them. See also later in Part I, Humanistic Associations with Architecture.
21 Air passenger numbers are increasing at the rate of 5% per year. The Airbus Industrie A380 project is due to make its first flight in 2002 and to enter service in 2006.
22 Lovelock himself is a strong advocate of technological improvement as a way of conserving the planet's ecology, including nuclear energy which he sees as a much smaller threat than the continued increase of carbon dioxide emissions. See James Lovelock, *Homage to Gaia: Life of an Independent Scientist*, Oxford University Press, Oxford, 2000.
23 Eric Loe, *The Value of Architecture*, RIBA Future Studies, London, 2000, p.51.
24 The lessons of traditional building concepts are explored in Part III, Vernacular Architecture.
25 This example is examined in more detail in Part III, Vernacular Architecture.
26 For a concise detailed summation of the manner in which building work was carried out in Roman times see Chapter 7, 'Materials, Techniques and Organisation' of J.B.Ward-Perkins, *The Severan Buildings of Lepcis Magna: An Architectural Survey*, Society for Libyan Studies, London, 1993.
27 Names appear in medieval records and in addition some buildings or elements of buildings are signed, either to ensure payment for the work or, less commonly, to identify the man with the work. For example at Little Moreton Hall, Cheshire, the great bay windows added to the building in 1559 are incised by their maker Richard Dale. See R.W.Brunskill, *Timber Building in Britain*, Victor Gollancz: London, 1985, p.34.
28 'Not only were nineteenth-century buildings shaped by new, complex requirements, social and technical, but they were commissioned by new types of patron. The growth of a strong middle class of professional and business men created a type of patron no longer likely to be familiar with matters of taste and architectural values. Nor was the architectural profession prepared to meet the inexorable tide of change described.' Sir Banister Fletcher, *A History of Architecture*, (18th ed), University of London, 1975, p.1124.
29 The Beaux-Arts system of architectural education 'conceived essentially as a preparation for the design of monumental public buildings' was founded in France in 1819 but based on the pre-revolutionary Académie Royale d'Architecture and was hugely influential throughout Europe in the eighteenth and nineteenth centuries. See David Watkin, *A History of Western Architecture*, Barrie & Jenkins: London, 1986, p.376.
30 Also see Part III, The Purpose of Technology in Architecture for John Ruskin and William Morris' influence on the development of ecological awareness in architecture and Part II for its relationship to the development of 'Pure architecture'.
31 For a detailed study of Joseph Paxton's Crystal Palace and Ferdinand Dutert's Palais des Machines see the essays by John McKean and Stuart Durant in *Lost Masterpieces*, Phaidon, London, 1999.
32 In Great Britain, courses in architecture began to appear from the 1830s – the Institute of British Architects was founded in 1834 (with a royal charter granted three years later), the Architectural Association was founded in 1847 in London, and the first university school of architecture was founded in 1894 in Liverpool. However, membership or attendance of any course offered was not a prerequisite to holding the title of architect. 'Pupilage, part-time courses and self-help, however, appear to have been the prime means of architectural education ....' Sir Banister Fletcher, *History of Architecture*, (18th ed), University of London, 1975, p.1125.
33 Mme. de Mandrot, who had been the host for this meeting, later invited Le Corbusier to design a house for her in La Pradet which she later condemned as 'absolutely uninhabitable'. Le Corbusier stated that she was not 'just right to live in a modern house'. C. St John Wilson, *The Other Tradition of Modern Architecture, Academy*, London, 1995, pp.13–14 and 102–109.
34 Reyner Banham, *Theory and Design in the First Machine Age*, Architectural Press, London, 1960, p.329.
35 Banham also believed that though the theory and aesthetics of the International Style were evolved from Futurism, their resolution was only achieved by drawing nearer to academic tradition, ibid. p.327.

36 Happily, there are recent signs in the UK of a revision of these building patterns, thanks to new Government policies based on Richard Rogers' report *Towards an Urban Renaissance, Final Report of the Urban Task Force*, E & F.N. Spon, London, 1999.
37 Robert Venturi, Denise Scott-Brown, Steve Izenour, *Learning from Las Vegas*, MIT Press, Cambridge, Mass.,1972 (revised ed., 1977), p.xii; Robert Venturi and Denise Scott-Brown, *Complexity and Contradiction in Architecture*, Museum of Modern Art, New York,1966. The Venturi's practice, Venturi, Rauch, Scott-Brown, has itself completed at least one building (Lewis Thomas Laboratories, Princeton, New Jersey) where their sole input has been to create the 100mm outer skin – the planning, design, detailing and specification having been created by others (in this case the Payette Company).
38 Tadao Ando, 'Towards New Horizons in Architecture' (1991) in K. Nesbitt, *Theorizing a New Agenda for Architecture,* Princeton Architectural Press, New York, 1996, p.458.
39 'A Life in the Day of Carolyn Grace', *Sunday Times Magazine*, 3 September 2000, p.54. It has been suggested that when people live in extreme situations their relationship with the machines that protect their existence deepens into an equal partnership where technology and humanity take on a form of symbiosis. See Rachel Armstrong (ed.), 'Space Architecture', *Architectural Design*, vol. 70, no.2, March 2000, p.5.
40 See Herbert Schiffer, *Shaker Architecture*, Schiffer Publishing, West Chester, Penn., 1979.
41 See David Nye, *Electrifying America*, MIT Press, Cambridge, Mass., 1990, p.238.
42 Low cost airline Easyjet first introduced Internet sales in 1998. Initially online reservations represented less than 1% of their total business, for the same period in 2000 it had risen to 76%. A telehotel is a building in which Internet based companies 'lodge' the hardware that facilitates their operation with access to constant maintenance and ideal environmental conditions.
43 Sir Norman Foster was architect for the redesign of the Reichstag in Berlin and Enrico Miralles for the Scottish Parliament in Edinburgh.
44 Probably not. David Watkin draws attention once more to Le Corbusier's influence in the emergence of Brutalist architecture comparing it to the *Béton brut* (raw, unfaced concrete) and exposed unfinished brick work of his later works in Marseilles, Paris and Chandigarh. David Watkin, *A History of Western Architecture*, Barrie & Jenkins, London, 1986, p.563.
45 Botand Bognar, 'From Ritualistic Objects to Science Fiction Constructs: The Enigma of Shin Takamatsu's Architecture' in Paolo Polledri (ed.), *Shin Takamatsu*, Rizzoli, New York, 1993. *Batman* was made at Pinewood Studios, England by Warner Brothers in 1989 and directed by Tim Burton. Furst was assisted by Nigel Phelps. Another powerful distopian city created on celluloid is the seemingly infinite 'Hades Landscape' designed for the 1982 film *Bladerunner* by Lawrence Paull, Syd Mead, Doug Trumbull in collaboration with the director Ridley Scott. For information on both these films see Dietrich Neumann (ed.), *Film Architecture: Set Designs from Metropolis to Bladerunner*, Prestel, Munich, 1999. The Ark, or Nishina Dental Clinic in Fushimi, Kyoto was built in 1981–82.
46 Tim Benton also makes this point in his comparison between totalitarian architecture and propaganda 'Speaking Without Adjectives' in the catalogue from the exhibition *Art and Power: Europe Under the Dictators 1930-45* organised by the Hayward Gallery, London, 26 October 1995–21 January 1996.
47 Jean Baudrillard, 'The Beaubourg-Effect: Implosion and Deterrence' (1977) in Neil Leach (ed.), *Rethinking Architecture: A Reader in Cultural Theory*, Routledge, London and New York, 1997, pp.210-11.
48 '… "on the earth" already means "under the sky." Both of these also mean "remaining before the divinities" and include a "belonging to men's being with one another." By a primal oneness the four – earth and sky, divinities and mortals – belong together in one.' Martin Heidegger from 'Building, Dwelling, Thinking' in Krell, *Heidegger,* p.351

PART 2

THEMES IN TECHNOLOGICALLY INSPIRED ARCHITECTURE

Many contemporary architects profess a lack of interest in 'style' and declare any attempt to place specific buildings into pigeonholes irrelevant. Indeed, the eclectic mix of contemporary architecture makes it difficult to define particular groupings. However, to understand the trends of a subject such as design which has such diverse influences, it is helpful to attempt some sort of clarification, as long as the examination is undertaken to disclose principles rather than to codify rules.[1] Having noted this concern, it is possible to identify a number of themes that are currently being explored in contemporary architecture which, if examined, may help engender a better understanding of its meaning. To explore a theme that appears in architectural form is not to categorise the buildings under examination, as several themes may be interplayed within the same project and be addressed in different ways by the design team. Also, thematic influence does not proscribe architectural form in the same way as does adherence to a particular style, as two buildings working towards and achieving a similar aim may still adopt different strategies and have a very different appearance.

It could be argued that technology is just one of a multitude of influences that can be identified in contemporary architecture; however, technological advance is so important that not only does it have a powerful individual effect, it is also a significant part of each one of the multitude. In different projects, varied issues will take precedence; culture, society, economy impacting on the form and image of the building design through indiscernible pressures as well as conscious design decisions. However, technology will also impact on every one of the countless choices that determine the final building product: the materials it is made from; the way it will be heated, cooled, lit; siting; access; security; all aspects of operation and maintenance. Where other aspects of the design brief are dominant, technology may not be so apparent but its influence will still be there. In some cases the concealment of this influence is important if the building is to do its job well, for example in a hospice the medical technology that enables the building to operate efficiently must be secondary to the comfortable domestic setting that will enable the patients to relax as much as possible in difficult circumstances. However, as technology becomes a recognisable component of all aspects of life, its presence in architecture is more frequently accepted as automatic, and its presence has become something not to be concealed but rather something overt, a part of the collective stimulus that makes the building.

Architectural form is wonderfully rich in its manifestation and, like other influences, the effect of technology can be expressed in many ways. Careful examination of this expression indicates that although form varies widely there is a discrete range of four thematic intentions, and the appearance of a design generally aspires to one of these, or sometimes, to a blend of more than one. These themes can respectively be entitled pop, pure, organic and tectonic. Pop architecture is a popular representation of the romantic image of advanced technology, pure architecture is a purist minimal response to the essence of technique and materiality, organic architecture is an interpretation of the way technology emerges from natural organic form, tectonic architecture is a celebration of the application of technology in the articulation of structure and component design. Many designers experienced in the use of new technology can and do make use of these different themes, varying their architectural form depending on design criteria, site, budget, program and client. Sometimes the expression of these themes can become the hallmark of a particular designer. Clients will recognise this particular expertise and commission the work on that basis, anticipating the sort of design they will get. For others, the theme emerges as a part of the response to the specific project, and in this case the designer may utilise the experience of engineers, contractors and manufacturers who have specialist knowledge of the field. Designing architecture is an immensely complex business, merging technical and aesthetic awareness in a synthesis that, because of the incredibly diverse functions of so many buildings, is more difficult than any other design field. Understanding the meaning behind this major component of design influence surely helps architects make better buildings. By exploring these themes it may be possible to reveal not only the way in which technology impacts the image of a building, but also the effect it has in placing architecture as a crucial manifestation of human activity.

POP ARCHITECTURE

The most simplistic manner in which technology can appear in building is through the visual representation of its characteristics. In order to do this effectively the desired connotations must be patently clear to those for whom the message is intended – ambiguity diffuses the image. The early root of twentieth-century popular architecture was originally to be found in the imagery (rather than the reality) of historical styles. Romantic reinterpretations of every period's buildings from the idyllic rural cottage to the Alpine *Schlöss* could be translated into palatial houses, office buildings, banks or town halls. Historicism was a source of novelty though in some cases there were philosophical or cultural underpinnings related to the search for a national identity or a connection with an earlier period in history which had nostalgic associations. Because pop architecture follows the trend rather than makes it, technology rarely figured as an inspiration until it too began to be associated with romance.

Turn of the century popular architecture in the USA was influenced by contemporary events – the Mexican Revolution inspired a wide-ranging reexamination of Latin and South American culture including prehistoric Inca and Toltec design favouring geometric and complex pattern making. Much of this work was purely decorative; however, Frank Lloyd Wright integrated this imagery with an innovative constructional

36 *Neuschwanstein, Bavaria by Eduard Riedel and his client King Ludwig II – a fairy-tale castle built in the nineteenth century and inspiration for Walt Disney in the twentieth.*

37 Frank Lloyd Wright, Ennis House, Los Angeles, 1924.

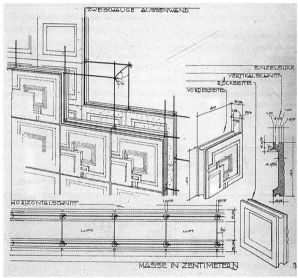

38 Frank Lloyd Wright, patented light-weight block walling system, 1923 used in La Miniatura, Freeman House, Ennis House and Storer House. Technical innovation coupled with a vibrant contemporary imagery.

39 1920s' Egyptian style shipping office, Chicago.

method utilising mechanical casting of concrete blocks into a series of houses near Los Angeles beginning in 1923. When Howard Carter discovered Tutankhamen's burial chamber in 1922, Egyptian motifs became a new decorative trend. But it was the excitement and romance of the machine, the ocean liner, the Streamliner train, the Zeppelin, the airliner and the fast car that had the most memorable technological stylistic influence. The seductive romance of travel conducted at speed in stylish, expensive modern machinery created a repertoire of imagery that became familiar, first through magazines and popular cinema, and then transferred into interior design, product design and architecture. If you were not among the privileged few who actually travelled in these vehicles you could at least use buildings that possessed the same glamorous associations.

The Futurist Movement, founded in 1909, comprised a group of artists, writers and designers whose work celebrated speed, modernity and machinery and condemned history and academic tradition. Though the Futurists were undoubtedly an influence on the incipient Modern Movement of the early 1920s they also inspired more popular styles and design trends. The heady musings of its main voices, Filippo Tomaso Marinetti and Antonio Sant'Elia, idealised the seductive qualities of technology. In the Futurist Manifesto of 1909 Marinetti stated:

> *We will sing of the midnight fervour of arsenals and shipyards blazing with electric moons; insatiable stations swallowing the smoking serpents of their trains; factories hung from the clouds by the twisted threads of their smoke; bridges flashing like knives in the sun, giant gymnasts that leap over rivers; adventurous steamers that scent the horizon, deep chested locomotives that paw the ground with their wheels, like stallions harnessed with steel tubing; the easy flight of aircraft, their propellers beating the wind like banners with a sound like the applause of a mighty crowd.*[2]

In 1914 Sant'Elia wrote in the preface to an exhibition catalogue including drawings of his evocative but mythical Cittá Nuova:

> *The problem of modern architecture is not a problem of rearranging its lines ... but to raise the new built structure on a sane plane, gleaning every benefit of science and technology ... . We must invent and rebuild ex novo our modern city like an immense and tumultuous shipyard, active, mobile and everywhere dynamic, and the modern building like a gigantic machine.*[3]

That Futurism is connected with pop architecture is undeniable – compare these statements with one by American designer Norman Bel Geddes: 'We enter a new era. We live and work under pressure with a tremendous expenditure of energy. We feel that our time is more urgent, complex, and discordant than life ever was before ... . Today, speed is the cry of our era, and greater speeds are the goals of tomorrow.'[4] Though the Futurists talked about rebuilding and recreating, their most lasting architectural legacy was the powerful evocative drawings of Sant'Elia's *Cittá futurista*.

Sant'Elia's death in the trenches in 1916 is a poignant epitaph to this movement that set freedom and imagination above harsh reality.[5]

The popular version of modern movement architecture, Streamline, and its variations such as Moderne, were clearly related to fashionable vehicle-inspired design. Rather than a response to a new architectural manifesto, this was a glamorous dressing up of conventional forms in sweeping curves with plain surfaces relieved by geometric patterns, plate glass, mirrors and chrome. Though this architecture is in many cases kitsch it is not without value. Art Deco is a relatively modern term coined in the

40 Sant'Elia, design for an Electric Power Station, 1914 (ink on paper).

42 The Art Deco Empire Diner, New York City.

41 Sant'Elia, Boccioni, Marinetti in uniform in 1916.

43 The Streamline Coca-Cola Bottling Plant moored in down-town Los Angeles by Robert V. Derrah, 1936–37.

44 The bonnet mascots are visible even from street level on the Chrysler Building, New York; William Van Allen, 1928–31.

1960s following a successful exhibition in Paris that focused on the 1925 'Exposition Internationale des Arts Décoratifs et Industriels Modernes'. The style was '... a reaction to the revolutions of our time – industrialisation, invention, communication and changes in society ... . It was pervasive, sweeping, democratic, and yet also elitist.'[6] Art Deco retains a vitality and exuberance that are admirable and in the best examples represent the aesthetic sense of the age better than almost anything else. William Van Allen's Chrysler Building of 1928–31 would not be so memorable were it not for the appliqué of giant chromium nickel steel eagle bonnet mascots and a ring of hubcaps and radiator grills around the 31st floor. The massive steel structure of the skyscraper, clad on the outside like the best Detroit heavy metal built by its client, resonates with the exuberance and confidence of the age, though paradoxically this building, like many of the USA's best Art Deco skyscrapers, was built at a time when the world economy was foundering under an incipient Depression that only a world war could fully dispel. 'True' modernists had little time for Art Deco – in his retrospective of the Bauhaus published in 1935 Walter Gropius took pains to distance the work from '... imitations which distorted the fundamental truth'.[7]

45 Norman Bel Geddes and Albert Kahn, General Motors Building, New York World's Fair, 1939.

Subsequent versions of pop architecture have drawn on other aspects of advanced technology as it has attracted public attention. International exhibitions drew together exuberant if inaccurate versions of remote cultures in strange juxtaposition in order to catch the imagination – the imagery has subsequently been transferred, primarily into the sort of commercial buildings where attracting the public is important. The image of future technology was a popular theme at Expos, one of the most memorable being the *Futurama* exhibit designed by Norman Bel Geddes for the General Motors Highways and Horizons Building at the 1939 World's Fair in New York City. Visitors rode on moving cars that encircled a vast diorama of the future American city – high-speed highways, skyscrapers, scientific farms and of course streamlined GM cars and trucks. Among other exhibits Raymond Loewy designed *Rocketport* for the Chrysler Corporation, a vision of future transportation in space during which visitors saw a rocket being launched. Loewy commented: 'people who saw it once often

46 Raymond Loewy's design for Rocketport *in the Chrysler Motors building, New York World's Fair, 1939.*

returned; it was a thrilling preview of what many believed could happen in the future.'[8] Though real space exploration did not get under way until the 1950s and 1960s, the potency of the idea led not only to the transferred imagery of spacecraft but to emulations of speculations on life in the future drawn from science fiction. Images of future life were communicated through magazines such as *Popular Mechanics*, *Ladies' Home Journal*, *House and Home*. People were also exposed to possible futures through the cinema, not only by science fiction but by set designers' ideas of what the ultra-modern home should look like, perhaps most famously in the 1949 filming of Ayn Rand's right-wing novel, *The Fountainhead*. Here Gary Cooper plays the uncompromising architect Howard Roark, who commits the ultimate act of architectural criticism by blowing up a building designed by him because the design has been changed without his knowledge.[9]

Enjoyable and amusing though many twentieth century pop culture inspired buildings are, there are relatively few that can be seen as more than the popcorn on the architecture menu. They helped create an image of the period to which the strongest contemporary response is nostalgia for a time when the potential of the future seemed glamorous and without threat. This nostalgia is partly based on the fact that it is difficult to identify a similar sort of pop architecture today. There are still many theme parks, restaurants and hotels that express the image of some sort of technological future in their make-up, but even a 10 year old can appreciate the cynicism of a tie-in to a current Hollywood blockbuster theme – the optimism of a general engagement with the excitement of science that was popular in the past is less likely to draw the punters today. In addition, the view of where we are headed in technological terms is less clear and there is always the sneaking suspicion that, wherever it is, it may not be universally recommended as a wholly positive destination. It is therefore much

47 Architect hero/villain Howard Roark from King Vidor's 1949 film, The Fountainhead.

more difficult for popular culture to tap into a recognisable image of the future that retains the excitement and romance it once had but avoids the possible diasporas that may also be waiting. Epcot technological theme park is now the least popular destination in the Florida Disney zone, its designers finding it difficult to update the displays that among other scientific miracles once confidently showed the human race off to populate the Solar System – for those who seek technological thrills it is a much more attractive proposition to drive down the road to Universal Studies and take the 'Back to the Future' ride.

The past is therefore a much safer place from which to draw influence today. Pop architecture always did raid the previous ages for ideas, but when the future is uncertain, history becomes an even more hospitable refuge. Kitsch reminders of past styles and pale imitations of exotic locations are now fashionable for some restaurant chains, for example; 'Johnny Rockets', a 1950s rock n' roll nostalgia trip; or 'Rainforest', plastic jungle with chlorinated waterfalls and piped bird song. This is safe architecture once more, apparently exuberant – but really anonymous because of its abandonment of contemporary inspiration. Such architecture is harmless in a theme park, but becomes insidious if present in every neighbourhood in competition with your local restaurant. The best pop architecture is quirky, individual, idiosyncratic. It draws on imagery in an honest, though perhaps naive manner. It is innocent and

48 Shopping mall jungle at the Rainforest Cafe.

enjoyable. It is not possible to create genuine examples of this sort of architecture cynically driven solely by commercial objectives. Great pop architecture is memorable and a cogent symbol of its place and age; if technology has been the inspiration, it expresses its influences with a powerful sensuousness. However, no matter how good pop architecture is, in order to achieve its aims there is absolutely no necessity for it actually to be technologically advanced.[10] Enjoy the ride, but if you are looking for the message it is better to look elsewhere.

PURE ARCHITECTURE

The stripping away of decorative elements from building is a core characteristic of much twentieth-century architecture and though the aesthetic opportunities in this design strategy were clear to the modernist architects, their primary inspiration was originally philosophical, founded in the belief that by removing everything that was not essential some basic truth about honesty to materials and form would be revealed. The initial inspiration for a pared down, simplistic design in twentieth-century architecture begins with the revelation of traditional Japanese design, images of which began to appear in the West after the opening up of the country for trade in the second half of the nineteenth century. As early as 1862, the Japanese exhibits at the International Exhibition in London were creating a stir among receptive designers such as E.W. Godwin, A.H. Mackmurdo and Christopher Dresser who published *Japan, its Architecture, Art and Art Manufacture* in 1882. Japanese architecture celebrates harmony with site and consciousness of materials, together with the development of an overlapping, free flowing space. It is the antithesis of formal nineteenth-century western architecture with its grand symmetry, highly decorated surfaces and separated rooms. Bruno Taut admired the 'cleanness' of Japanese architecture and, significantly, Frank Lloyd Wright acknowledged its influence not in terms

49 A.H. Mackmurdo, exhibition stand for the Century Guild at Liverpool International Exhibition, 1886.

50 Japanese interior, Kyoto.

of construction or form but in its 'elimination of the insignificant'.[11] However, it is important to note that though twentieth-century architects were attracted by the Japanese methods of using materials, modules and space, it was because what they had seen accorded with their own desires rather than indicating an involvement with its underlying philosophical significance.

The appearance of Japanese architecture was, however, a catalyst for the free thinking architects who were beginning to envisage a more simple architectural environment based on site and brief, structure and materials, light and form. This rejection of traditional architectural styles began simultaneously throughout Europe and North America towards the end of the nineteenth century. International design journals such as the *Studio* magazine and influential publications such as Herman Muthesias' book *Das Englische Haus* encouraged cross cultural influences between locations separated widely by distance and language.[12] The Secessionist Movement in Vienna was influenced by the British Arts and Crafts Movement and the Glasgow Style (in particular the furniture, interiors and building designs of the architect Charles Rennie Mackintosh) in its move away from the decadent establishment to a celebration of the artist and the craftsman. This was a time when the coming together of powerful concepts, gifted designers and an effective medium for international communication meant that British ideas influenced the course of modern architecture.[13] Otto Wagner, a successful established Viennese architect found new inspiration in the ideas of the younger architects and designers he brought into his office, and fostered a move away from fashionable, romantic, historically inspired decorated confections

51 The Post Office Bank, Vienna; Otto Wagner 1904–8.

52 Warm air heating outlet in the Post Office Bank.

to a more simple, expressive, modern style. These newer buildings, though still highly decorated, expressed materials more honestly and in some cases were genuinely innovative. Wagner's Post Office Bank, though clad in stone, expressed the bronze fixings as part of the articulation of the facade. Internally the banking hall lay at the base of an atrium with a double layer glazed roof whose simple form and constructional support were the main form of decoration. Lighting details, desks and air conditioning outlets were created from simple, expressive, mechanically inspired forms.

The Viennese architect Adolf Loos originally allied himself with the Secessionists but broke away in the 'battle over language'. Loos had been born in Brno, studied at Dresden Polytechnic, and toured the USA before settling in Vienna in 1896. He believed that the Classical form was at the root of all architecture – in his 1910 essay *Arkitectur* he stated: 'I saw how the ancients had built and I saw how century after century, year after year, they had been emancipated from ornamentation.

53 Adolf Loos, Steiner House, Vienna, 1910.

Consequently, I had to take up from the point at which the chain had been broken. One thing I knew: to stay on the track of this development I had to become still more simple.'[14] His architecture sought to express a functional coherence through spatial economy and an absence of ornament. Loos was as influential in his writing as in his building design; his most famous attack on architectural ornament: 'Ornament is crime, like a tattoo on the human body; a sign of degeneration' was delivered in his 1908 essay *Ornament und Verbrechen* (*Ornament and Crime*) and was reiterated in a range of published work over the first two decades of the twentieth century, his essay on this subject being published in the journal edited by Le Corbusier, *L'Esprit Nouveau* in 1920.[15] Loos' ideas developed from a search for the expression of the simplicity of form into a quest for an anti-architecture in which he urged that the 'building should be dumb on the outside and reveal its worth on the inside.'[16] Perhaps his most influential project was never built; the 1922 entry for the *Chicago Tribune* Building competition (won by a pseudo-Gothic steel framed skyscraper) was a build-

54 Adolf Loos, entry for the 1922 Chicago Tribune *architectural competition.*

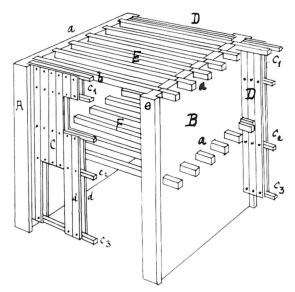

55 Adolf Loos' design for an economical construction system aimed primarily at public housing that limits the necessity for foundations to fire walls. Loos patented the idea while still working at the Vienna Housing Department in 1921 at around the same time that he was developing his Chicago Tribune *competition entry.*

ing without decoration, its form derived solely from its enigmatic shape, a 120-metre tall polished black granite Doric column. Loos stated the reason for choosing such a remarkable form was that the brief required a building that would be immediately associated with the *Chicago Tribune* and the city in which it was built. The building could not do this by attempting to be larger or higher than its competitors because whatever its proportions they would soon be exceeded. Significantly, he speculated on adopting the new forms of modern architecture: 'There remains yet another idea, that of adopting the new architectural forms without any traditional basis ... . However, these non-traditional forms are rapidly supplanted by others, or the proprietors complain that they are out of fashion, since the fashion in forms changes very frequently, just like that of clothing.'[17] Loos stated that he had chosen the column because it embodied 'tradition'; however, by placing it out of context it simultaneously is familiar in form but a challenge to convention – it is therefore an example of what he described as an alternative response to 'universal architectural language'.

In its gestation period, the search for pure form was one of the prime issues that concerned the leading protagonists of the Modern Movement. However, this ambition seemed to become less important as the movement gained momentum. Machine age doctrines came under pressure from the necessity to make more complex use of space and materials as the relatively simple functions of the early projects gave way to larger, more complex building types. Mies van der Rohe moved to Berlin when he was 16 to be apprenticed to the architect Peter Behrens. His early work strongly refers to Loos' influence, and though he was also inspired by Classical architecture (in particular by the German neoclassical architect Schinkel, whose impressive austere buildings were readily accessible in the capital) he also readily embraced the potential of technology to shape future architectural form. In his address to the Illinois Institute of Technology in 1950 he stated: 'Technology is rooted in the past. It dominates the present and tends into the future. It is a real historical movement – one of the great movements which shape our present epoch.'[18] Mies' early buildings, in particular the Barcelona Pavilion of 1929, brought space, form, light and materiality

56 Karl Friedrich Schinkel, Altes Museum, Berlin, 1824–8.

57 and 58
Barcelona Pavilion,
Mies van der Rohe,
1929.

together in a masterful orchestration that seemed to express the art of architecture simultaneously with an evocation of the new technology becoming available. This was signified in part through materials like the chromed steel of the cruciform columns and the large planes of glass, but also through the structure in cantilevers and free standing walls. In order to create such an immaculately assembled building discipline was essential, though in this case it did not form a straitjacket to creativity – more traditional materials such as marble and stone were specified too, their characteristic surfaces and patterns enhanced by the highly defined planes and volumes into which they were shaped.[19] If there was a peak of early Modernism this building, originally intended to be a temporary pavilion at an international expo, was it. Mies' later designs increasingly become formal exercises, focused on symmetry and balance, restricted in material innovation – ultimately they become anonymous and autocratic.[20] This later work utilises a 'method' to create form – the concentration on the use of open space and transparent walls regardless of function compromises the operation of the buildings and subjugates the individual to the dominance of the architectural idea, removing in some cases their rights to privacy and comfort.

If western architecture was influenced by Japan in the latter part of the nineteenth century there can be no doubt that the reverse was true in the second part of the twentieth. The catastrophic aftermath of the Pacific war led to a complete revolution in Japanese culture as it was inducted into the sphere of western influence. By the 1970s the country had completed a remarkable technological revolution that turned it into a manufacturing power house that would soon challenge the economic dominance of the USA and Europe. The Japanese architect Tadao Ando has been compared to both Mies van der Rohe and Adolf Loos, but his architecture, though inspired by western Modernism, does not forsake traditional Japanese concepts. Born in Osaka in 1941, Ando was educated in building crafts and had an eclectic personal history, spending part of his time as a professional boxer and travelling widely before settling to architecture. The intrinsic appreciation of materiality essential in Japanese traditional architecture is transformed in Ando's philosophy into a new understanding of industrial building materials such as reinforced concrete, steel and glass. Ando describes these as 'authentic' materials and admires their capacity to be used in their pure form, exposed and undisguised. Ando's best buildings also express a quest for pure formal geometry, which he describes as 'the base or framework that endows architecture with presence'.[21] Despite the overt modernity and man-made character of these buildings they are remarkably sensitive to site – the natural world surrounds the constructed artefacts, intensifying the holistic architectural experience. This is a clear evocation of traditional Japanese sensitivities to nature which is remade to be part of the manufactured world – nature, endowed by humanity with a new rational order. 'I seek to instil the presence of nature within an architecture austerely constructed by means of transparent logic. The elements of nature – water, wind, light, and sky – bring architecture derived from ideological thought down to the ground level of reality and awaken man-made life within it.'[22] Ando's architecture above all things expresses a sense of spirituality which is paradoxically connected with the human understanding that it is only the man-made object that can reveal the special meaning of the inhabited world. This is why his marriage chapels – which have limited religious connotations as they exist primarily as fashionable additions to hotels to allow young Japanese people to have a western style wedding – still possess such a sense of spiritual presence. Impeccably made cast concrete, steel and glass have been arranged to shape light, sound and temperature to the optimum settings that allow human sensitivity to a sense of place to be realised.

59 and 60
Wedding Chapel, Mount Rokko, Osaka, Tadao Ando.

Despite the many cultural and environmental differences between Loos, Mies and Ando, they exhibit a number of common factors that have enabled them at different stages in their careers to create an architecture that comes close to defining the essence of pure architectural form. Though they all acknowledged their debt to Classical architecture they also all sought to express the spirit of their age in architecture via an intimate engagement with materiality. It is perhaps significant that for each designer his best buildings are relatively small. The intimate, domestic size architecture is refreshing because of the consummate control that has clearly been maintained – the design is good because of what is left out, rather than what is left in. When the attempt to make pure form is enlarged beyond this domestic scale it can easily become simplistic and dominant rather than subservient to human presence. The formulaic apartment spaces of Mies' Lake Shore Drive skyscraper apartments in Chicago have long since been altered by owners, breaking through walls and floors to create individual, personally tuned dwellings that still make the most of that great view of Lake Michigan.[23] The current trend in minimal design is also largely restricted to the domestic and has been described as a response to the confusion and complexity of daily life. However, in many cases, along with the clutter, it could be argued that minimalist buildings have also lost comfort and personality. It is probable that many clients are subjugating their lifestyles to the restrictive dictates of their architects in the search for fashion rather than aesthetic simplicity. Is a minimalist house an

61 Lake Shore Drive Apartments, Chicago, Mies van der Rohe.

expression of the inhabitant's taste or the designer's? Architecture is an art form that engages with the inhabitant as a collaborator, for without the client and the user purpose is absent and architecture without purpose is ultimately sterile and redundant. The joke about the arrogant architect who chooses the colour of his client's slippers is too old still to be funny.[24] In *Ornament and Crime* Loos describes a satirical tale of the client who has a *Gesamtkunstwerk* house designed for him. The architect visited him at home and immediately exclaimed, ' "What kind of slippers are those you've got on?"... The master of the house looked at his embroidered slippers. Then he breathed in relief. This time he felt quite guiltless. The slippers had been made to the architect's original designs. So he answered in a superior way. "But Mr Architect! Have you already forgotten? You yourself designed them!" "Of course," thundered the architect, "but for the bedroom! They completely disrupt the mood here with these two impossible spots of colour. Can't you see that?" Loos could summon a remarkable amount of vitriol to chastise the ad-hoc theft of historic decorative images to dress up buildings, but even he allowed his clients to have a picture of their children on the piano.

ORGANIC ARCHITECTURE

The authority of the natural world over the man-made is consummate, though it is a part of the human psyche sometimes to disregard this fact. The basis of construction materiality is that even the most artificial component emerges from the raw product, though the process that leads to the end result determines the relationship that the artificial has with the natural. Recognisably natural materials have a presence based on human experience that is tested, safe and sure. They have a realness, a grounding in the world, which is recognisable and identifiable. They have a rapport with human beings because we believe, even if this is not always true, that we can identify their source. To know what something is made of is to recognise its history. The primal natural materials are very few and are intimately related to location – in western Europe there are perhaps just two: stone and wood. To these we can begin to add a secondary manufactured layer that has become tested through long use: thatch, brick, plaster, cement, glass. In some parts of the world grass is a primary natural material, in others mud. As technology has led to the development and introduction of new materials our human response to their presence has been established, then has evolved. As already discussed, in order to determine his personal response to architecture, Tadao Ando has identified with a group of contemporary materials which he has labelled 'authentic'. He then composes them with a sensitivity redolent of traditional Japanese architecture. The essence of the spaces he creates has a remarkable resonance with buildings from an earlier period, a link established through the interpretation of space, light and site rather than building image. However, he does not copy traditional forms; the architectural form is different because the materials he uses have different capabilities and therefore afford different opportunities.

The nineteenth-century French architect Eugene Viollet-le-Duc was one of the first to try to express the true nature of modern building. A life-long enemy of the establishment institutions of the Ecole des Beaux-Arts and the Académie he believed the functional legacy of Gothic to be the only precedent that a modern architect required. As early as 1863 he wrote:

> *In architecture, there are two necessary ways of being true. It must be true according to the* programme *and true according to the* methods of construction. *To be true according to the programme is to fulfil exactly and simply the conditions imposed by need; to be true according to the methods of construction, is to employ the materials according to their qualities and properties ... purely artistic questions of symmetry and apparent form are only secondary conditions in the presence of our dominant principles.*[25]

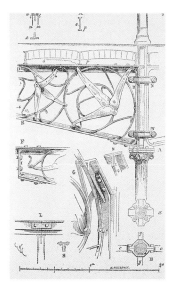

62 Cast and wrought iron detail from Viollet-le-Duc's Entretiens, *1872.*

Though Viollet's designs can be criticised as aesthetically crude, they also possess an undeniable novelty of form that indicates his involvement in a challenging search for a new type of architecture that integrated construction and form – a rationalist approach to design that would result in building patterns that employed contemporary structural systems as a spatial ordering force. Viollet-le-Duc was also a believer in the importance of creating a regionally identifiable architecture, an ambition he shared with a number of European architects at this time.[26] Another Frenchman, Hector Guimard, whose master Anatole de Baudot had been a pupil of Viollet-le-Duc, designed buildings which incorporated carved stone and wood in flowing sinuous shapes that resembled the living, growing asymmetry of nature. Though Guimard and Viollet have been described as structural rationalists, the forcing of such materials into these contorted shapes can hardly be seen as rational. However, it is significant that it was in their response to the relatively new materials of cast and wrought iron where their ambitions were most successful. The plastic nature of industrially worked metal was fully exploited until the resultant forms acquired the genuine sense of being crossbreed between organic filament and manufactured object. Probably the most famous and most powerful evocations of this approach to design are Guimard's Paris Métro stations, which made use of mass-produced, interchangeable cast iron and glass components to create evocative, energetic flowering structures that emerge from the earth, glowing with artificial light. Such structures are simultaneously technological and decorative, organic and machine-like.

63 Castle Beranger, Paris, Hector Guimard, 1894–95.

In the USA, Louis Sullivan pioneered a New World version of organic Expressionism that was married to the dynamic structural possibilities of steel. In 1892 Sullivan wrote a treatise called *Ornament in Architecture* in which he proclaimed '... ornament is mentally a luxury, not a necessity.'[27] Yet he also stated that the employment of decorative forms was 'an expression of life force'. This apparent contradiction is clarified in the presence of the architecture as Sullivan's immensely complex swirling and intricately decorated cast metal panels are deployed on the facade of his buildings within a completely rational pattern that expresses its regular structural grid. They form a tertiary layer to the structure and cladding that communicates both richness of purpose and a clear identity. Though there are recognisable stylised elements

64 Paris Métro Station, Hector Guimard, 1899–1904.

65 Carson Pirie Scott Department Store, Chicago, Louis Sullivan, 1899–1904.

from nature in Sullivan's decoration, the complexity and geometry of the patterning are so rich that they transcend representation and become an interpretation of the organic. Frank Lloyd Wright, who trained under Sullivan in Chicago and affectionately referred to him as his 'Lieber Meister', saw the 'organic' object as synonymous with the 'natural' and his description of the 'organic simplicity' which was his objective sounds remarkably like the *Gesamtkunstwerk* of the Secessionists.[28] In his book *The Natural House* (1954) Wright describes both the philosophical and pragmatic approach to building which he pursued both for his wealthy clients and the Usonian dwellings he intended for large-scale economic building.

> ... The ideal of 'organic simplicity' seen as the countenance of perfect integration ... naturally abolished all fixtures, rejected the old furniture, all carpets and most hangings, declaring them to be irrelevant or superficial decoration. The new practice made all furnishings so far as possible (certainly the electric lighting and heating systems) integral parts of the architecture. So far as possible all furniture was to be designed in place as part of the building. Hangings, rugs, carpets, were they to be used (as they might be if properly designed), all came into the same category.[29]

However, Wright did not restrict his inspiration from the organic to the sinuous form of the plant but saw it more generally as a model for integrating structure and construction into surface decoration: 'Architecture should strive to imitate the principles of nature without imitating its forms' and though like Loos he felt uneasy with the idea of 'ornament', like Sullivan he saw no reason to abandon the use of decoration in architecture provided it was fully integrated into the building fabric in a similar way to how it is found in nature.

> Heretofore, I have used the word 'pattern' instead of the word ornament to avoid confusion or to escape the passing prejudice. But here now ornament is in its place. Ornament meaning not only surface qualified by human imagination *but imagination giving* natural pattern *to structure* ... . This resource – integral ornament – is new in the architecture of the world.[30]

To Wright the organic was something quintessentially natural and therefore original, undiluted, pure – 'organic' as another version of the 'authentic'.

That such richly decorated, fluidic and complex buildings could be built within the same decade, and be inspired by the same material innovations as were the proto-modernists such as Adolf Loos, is both remarkable and typical of the contradictions that the introduction of new technologies engenders. However, the understanding that differing responses could each contain some validity within their very different forms was hardly possible at the time. For instance, Loos' opinion of Art Nouveau architecture was typically forthright: 'I tell you that the time will come when the furnishing of a prison cell by Professor Van de Velde will be considered an aggravation of the sentence.'[31] Le Corbusier too felt that there was but one route to the goal of modernity

66 Wingspread, *Wisconsin, the last of the great prairie houses by Frank Lloyd Wright, 1937.*

and that was through revolution in architecture if not in society itself! In the conclusion of *Vers une Architecture* he wrote: 'If we set ourselves against the past, we are forced to the conclusion that the old architectural code, with its mass of rules and regulations evolved during four thousand years, is no longer of any interest; it no longer concerns us: all the values have been revised; there has been revolution in the conception of what Architecture is.'[32] In the search for a polemical vision of modernity in architecture the concept that there could be many futures, each responding to different agendas, locations and technologies, was too anarchical to sustain. In reviewing the revolution of the Modern Movement in 1957 Alvar Aalto said, '... like all revolutions, begins with enthusiasm and ends in some form of Dictatorship'.[33] The shared aesthetic vision of the International Style architects was reinforced by the belief that theirs was the correct vision to the exclusion of all others.[34]

If the plasticity of cast metals provided special impetus to the expression of the organic in architecture, reinforced concrete allowed for even more dynamic possibilities. The exploitation of the potential of reinforced concrete design was undertaken by a series of gifted engineer architects who combined technical ability with aesthetic vision. Early reinforced concrete buildings had mimicked known forms like stonework and timber frames but the possibilities of creating replacements for longer span beams and trusses and then panel systems in which the structure became integral with the skin soon began to be exploited. The Mexican designer Felix Candela recognised the inherent strength of structural forms found in nature such as shells, and from 1951 created a series of increasingly more ambitious and evocative forms based on pure geometry though still reminiscent of the natural structure of eggs and sea shells. The American architect Eero Saarinen exploited the expressive potential of concrete further, particularly in his airport buildings in New York and Washington. The TWA terminal (1956–62) in New York is not only

67 Eero Saarinen, TWA terminal, New York, 1956–62.

organic in form, it seems to evoke the essence of flight with shapes reminiscent of eagle's wings, talons and a beak. Nevertheless, though the form is highly expressive it is not imitative. This building also exploits the ability of concrete to be used to create a complete three-dimensional form, the inside surface of the building following the outside envelope. This visually simulates the structural form of an animal which contains the compressive elements (bones) and tensile elements (muscles and tendons) within a smooth skin. The Washington Dulles building (1958–62) is different – formal, rectangular and almost Classical in plan, yet in section an elevating airfoil that rises from the passenger arrival point towards the airfield. The transparent, glazed vertical perimeter cladding allows the structural form to be revealed as if it is suspended in space. Whether the expression of this building is organic or tectonic is a moot point as the two influences merge here into one – is the airfoil reminiscent of the wing of a bird or an aircraft?[35]

The contemporary architect/engineer who is most renowned for his exploitation of the essence of the organic in structure is Santiago Calatrava. Born in 1951 in Valencia, Spain, Calatrava first took his architecture degree there before completing an engineering degree in Zurich. Calatrava has worked extensively in all the major structural materials – steel, concrete, wood – but has also created a number of more experimental projects exploiting new materials such as plastics based membranes and glass reinforced concrete. One facet of Calatrava's work is that he seeks to

68, 69, and 70
Glass reinforced concrete kinetic sculpture by Calatrava for the Museum of Modern Art in 1993.

exploit that pivotal point in structure that demarcates the line between balance and imbalance. His structures seem to capture a feeling of dramatic tension similar to that moment of uncertainty before stability, captured in the instant when a gull sweeps down to the ocean to catch a fish then soars once more into the air. As well as bridges and building designs he has created a number of kinetic devices that feature moving structural elements which accentuate not only the form of the members but the crucial importance of the joint as a pivot, a place which focuses forces. This same idea is present in static structures but expressed much more clearly in his kinetic experiments like the opening segmented roof of the Kuwait pavilion at Expo '92 in Seville, or the New York Museum of Modern Art's moving garden sculpture.

The expression of nature in man-made objects can so easily become kitsch because the building that tries too hard to be like an animal or a plant can easily become amusing rather than impressive. As Frei Otto stated: 'Technical objects such as a house do not become natural by imitating bird forms found in living nature or by using so called biological building materials.'[36] However, nature is a remarkable source of inspiration in establishing the meaning of contemporary architecture. Nature is not wasteful, its systems are self-designing, self-evaluating and constantly developing in order to combat change and redundancy. Remarkably, all the systems we look on as man-made can also be found in nature: hydraulics, pneumatics, geometric and cellular structures. Some are much stronger in nature than have been achieved artificially.[37] Science has always used nature as a resource, not only for gaining further knowledge about the universe but also to develop applied technology. However, humanity has an intimate relationship with the natural world that goes beyond our use of it; we are part of it too. Physically to manifest our presence in nature through building is to reveal a part of our existence. In order to reveal something new about the way architecture works in the natural world, the source of the technology must be understood, and revealed in built form. The most convincing organic architecture does this by seeking out the essence of natural form, either in materiality or structure, and reinterpreting it for a functional purpose – it is learning from nature, rather than exploiting it.

TECTONIC ARCHITECTURE

Within the previous thematic responses we have seen that the use of new technology in architecture has been synthesised with other ideas about fashion, aesthetics and nature. However, some contemporary architecture utilises advanced technology as the key element in determining the visual and spatial character of the building and celebrates it in an overt manner. High-Tech is a term that was first coined in the 1980s with reference to an architecture that overtly expressed the contemporary materials and techniques that were used in its construction. Charles Jencks attempted to list the characteristics of High-Tech with a mixture of stylistic, technical and cultural tags: inside-out; celebration of process; transparency; layering and movement; bright flat colours; a lightweight filigree of tensile membranes; optimistic confidence in a scientific culture. Though the term is relatively recent it already appears too proscriptive to describe such a wide range of buildings with incredibly differing ambitions.[38] The term tectonic acknowledges the designers' direct response to the challenge of expressing advanced construction techniques but does not seek to define the visual imagery they must exhibit, irrespective of the building's function.

Typical tectonic architecture usually features exposed elements of structure, the building skin defined as a separate element, and parts of the services expressed as elements in the formal composition. The building will appear energetic, dynamic, even incomplete. Indeed, the restless imagery of this architecture is directly related to a main reason architects give for exposing and separating elements of structure and services in this way: to create a flexible adaptive environment by allowing the interior to exist as a discrete operating unit while building maintenance and/or changes go on undisturbed outside.

The characteristics of tectonic architecture can be identified wherever the designer has become totally engaged in the potential of the construction technology to the extent that other stylistic concerns have become superfluous. Richard Buckminster Fuller, the American innovator, designer and proselytiser for the benefits of technological advance eschewed style in the design process, putting concern for materiality and techniques in the service of the programme above all else. Immediately after the Second World War Fuller convinced many Americans that the future house would be factory made, providing high quality, built-in servicing at reduced cost. His Wichita

71 Wichita House, Beech Aircraft Company, Buckminster Fuller, 1946.

House, to be constructed by the Beech Aircraft Company in a factory made redundant after war production ceased, took the form of a shiny, circular, aluminium drum that bore no relation to the typical North American dwelling. Its materials, volume and structure were all expressed in its form as was the ventilation operated by a large rotating fin on the roof. Thirty-seven thousand orders were received based purely on prelaunch journal articles and photographs, but Fuller's unwillingness to delegate production responsibility decisions to the industrialists who would carry out the task meant the project never went beyond the prototype stage.[39]

High technology does not always mean high cost; just as Fuller's Wichita House was an attempt to improve standards while reducing cost, Charles and Ray Eames' house of 1947–48 utilised standard industrialised building components assembled in a sensitive manner to make a seductive 'art' house. Built as part of publisher John Entenza's Case Study House program, the construction process was comparatively economical, but more importantly it showed that beautiful buildings could be made from cheap, mechanically produced components.[40] Though the Eames built few other buildings, the influence of this house, widely publicised in the *Art + Architecture* journal and then subsequently picked up for publication around the world, was enormous. The overriding aesthetic message that the Eames' design conveyed was of an assembled building. The materials and components are clearly defined and remain separate though harmonising into a coherent whole. This separateness of elements of structure, cladding, access, and services is crucial in understanding the elements of the architecture – it is a made object, and the message of its making, if not the detail, is understandable to all. The building also expresses flexibility, because if one can see immediately that the components are assembled, it is not too difficult to imagine them disassembled to allow change to take place, even if in reality this might not happen.[41]

72 Charles and Ray Eames pose in 1949 on the newly erected frame of their Case Study House in Pacific Palisades, California.

73 A recent photograph of the Eames house.

The Eames' house remains influential to this day and there have been many projects built all around the world that continue to explore the theme of the aesthetically assembled building. Cedric Price's influential Fun Palace project took this process one step further, integrating building components, structure and more humble functional shelter items, such as proprietary site cabins, into a multi-use, easily changeable community facility in Camden Town, London.[42] Both the Eames and Price were profoundly influential on the Archigram group whose ideas, though primarily created on paper, influenced a generation of young designers in the 1960s and 1970s. Peter Cook, Warren Chalk, Ron Herron, Michael Webb and Peter Greene created a world of flexible, portable, technology-inspired built environments which they communicated to the world through the magazine *Archigram*. Their experimental ideas directly influenced Richard Rogers and Renzo Piano who designed the first really high profile High-Tech building, the Beaubourg Cultural Centre. Their design, which was engineered by Peter Rice at Ove Arup, was the winner of a competition for a public arts and culture centre in Paris instigated by the French president Georges Pompidou. The building burst on to the world in an almost unprecedented blaze of publicity for a contemporary building and was immediately hugely controversial. Panned by much of the establishment press, the public loved it, breaking all predictions for visitor numbers. It was and still is an exuberant, dynamic and breathtakingly audacious building, slotted into the old city like a Formula I engine into a horse and buggy.[43]

Its structure is a framework for a complex network of multicoloured service pipes overlaid with constantly moving people carriers: lifts and escalators. But the building also employs pertinent urban design tactics by raising the accommodation into a single seven floor element along one side of the site, creating a new square which can be viewed from the many public access areas on the facing elevation. In turn, this allows the building to be viewed in its entirety as a backdrop to the activities in the square. Almost immediately, it could be seen that the building was to have a cataly-

74 As well as a building the architects created a place. Beaubourg Centre, Paris, Richard Rogers and Renzo Piano.

tic effect in bringing new life to a previously run-down area of the city as first restaurants and shops were built in new and existing buildings to service the visitors, then offices and housing were created in what was now a newly fashionable district. The Beaubourg Centre was the first overtly High-Tech building to grab world attention and prove that people had no prejudices in accepting innovative building form as long as it did its job properly.

Tectonic architecture is sometimes criticised as 'boys' toys' architecture, influenced by the science fiction comics of the 1950s, 1960s and 1970s and building toys like Meccano and Lego.[44] It is generally acknowledged that all children possess natural creativity which can be either nurtured or stifled by their developmental experiences. The experience of constructional toys may have influenced designers' enthusiasms for assembled buildings. However, if this is the case it should also be acknowledged that this might also help create a referential link for the general public because many more people made houses and bridges with construction sets and toy blocks as children than ever went on to become architects and make them as adults.

As intriguing as early childhood impressions might have been, it is probable that the more fundamental influences on tectonic architecture emerge from contemporary technological advance and (perhaps more so than in any other form of architecture) in the transfer of technological advance from one field to another. Building design is influenced by imagery from other diverse fields of technological activity such as cars, trains, aviation, and maritime design, industry, bridge building, and the military. However, in some cases the actual technology that has been developed for such applications has also impacted on the way buildings are built. Though such technology may be applied in many forms of architecture it is in tectonic architecture that this impact is most visible. Because these designs use technology as a main influence in defining image, they make clear that there is a connection between the way that architecture and the rest of the world's technology is developing. If the design expresses that technology in an accurate and appropriate manner, it locates architecture within the main thrust of progress and maintains its relevance in supporting the way we intend to inhabit the world of tomorrow.

75 *'Skyscrapers' at Cape Canaveral, Florida.*

76 *Shinkansen train, Japan.*

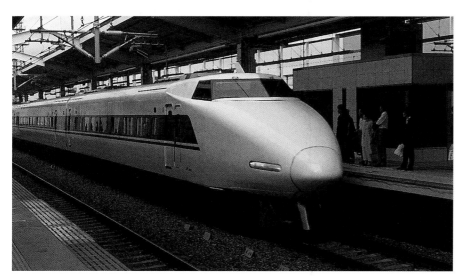

The British architect Nicholas Grimshaw seeks inspiration from the design of other large scale, complex objects. He compares the design of buildings to the design of boats, though it is not necessarily their appearance or their associations with the romance of travel that excites him but the operational features of the vehicle as an independent object: 'I like buildings to respond in the way a boat responds to the wind ... We have to start thinking of building things with life and vitality, as objects that can be used and changed, that can be made out of good materials if they are to be ephemeral. However long they last, they must be thoughtful, responsive mechanisms rather than dead, static monuments.'[45]

Although tectonic architecture does not attempt to duplicate romantic fashionable imagery as in pop architecture, other often quite diverse connotations can be made with the building form. Grimshaw's building for the *Western Morning News* in Plymouth sits on an elevated site above this port city that is the base of the Royal Navy, and because of its siting and the maritime connotations of the place a range of imagery can be associated with its curving metal structure, masts and glazed press hall. Ideas about ships, both square rigged and engine powered, are inevitable, but also one thinks of lighthouses and radar stations. Grimshaw acknowledges that the vision of a warship frequently seen in Plymouth Sound is an influence but only in that it is also 'a bold purposeful thing, finely engineered and with nothing that is superfluous'.[46]

77 Conceptual sketch drawn in 1990 by Nicholas Grimshaw of the Western Morning News Building, Plymouth, 1992.

Eagle Rock House by Ian Ritchie is another building that conjures up diverse images in the observers' attempt to define the building's character. The house sits in a heavily wooded site overlooked by the eagle shaped rock that gives it its name. The plan form (which is more pertinent than usual because the building can be seen from above) is laid out like an aircraft with fuselage, wings and tail, though this is where the direct reference to flight ends. Instead the building is made of a delicate steel frame, glass, and opening panels that admit the surrounding vegetation to the inside as well as allowing views of and reflecting the sky. The ultimate feeling is of an ephemeral, lightweight structure dropped into the site, a shelter sensitive to the location rather than a structure imposed on it.[47]

New technology is not always high-tech; a new use for a low-tech material can be just as challenging. Though tectonic architecture can take many forms – dramatic and bold like the *Western Morning News* building or subtle and reclusive like Eagle Rock House, it does not always consist of shiny metals, nuts and bolts and glass. New technology is making it possible to use materials such as quickly grown green wood saplings or recycled paper, which previously have not been regarded as suitable for making buildings. Work by the School of Woodland Industry, architects Ahrends, Burton and Koralek, and engineers Buro Happold in association with Frei Otto has resulted in a new form of construction integrating home grown roundwood timber of relatively small dimensions (50–200mm diameter) into a new structural system that enables large permanent buildings to be erected at relatively low cost using natural materials that can be grown quickly. Though the UK currently imports 80% of its building timber it actually produces enough wood to be self-sufficient; the problem is qual-

78 Eagle Rock House, Ian Ritchie, 1980

ity – only 10% of the trees planted will be grown to the size for conventional use, the rest are thinnings removed to control the quality and growth of the remainder, which is typically used for low value products like particle board, fuel or pulp. The project at Hooke Park in Dorset aims to find new methods of working with an old material – wet wood – using new jointing methods with epoxy resin and steel bars. Sawing of structural timber is avoided as it wastes material – it is also carefully graded by size for its job in compression, tension or as a composite member made up from a number of pieces. Part of the intention is also to build simply, without elaborate plant or difficult to acquire skills. The buildings created by this method show a new architectural language that reflects a material which is expected to move as it dries out, the timber is exposed internally and externally wherever possible and catenary rooves have been adopted that acknowledge both the tendency of slender timber to bend but also its substantial strength in tension.

79 Construction site at the School of Woodland Industry, Hooke Park, Dorset. New buildings from 'unusable' wet timber by Frei Otto, Buro Happold and Ahrends Burton and Koralak.

The Japanese architect Shigeru Ban has developed building systems using recycled paper made into tube forms for both structure and cladding. First used to make temporary shelters in the wake of the Kobi earthquake, the system has been developed into a family of products capable of constructing larger buildings with a wide range of uses. EXPO architecture always provides a particular conundrum for designers, how to create a building of significant quality which will represents its sponsors well but which will be redundant when the show is over in six months time. At Hanover 2000, Ban cooperated with Frei Otto and Buro Happold to design the world's first large scale building utilising locally collected recycled paper made into a woven basket-like paper tube structure as a main component. The foundation was made from a steel frame and scaffolding boards filled with sand, and the roof membrane – in part also made from paper, is reusable.

80 Post earthquake temporary housing made from recycled paper tubes, beer crates and plastic membrane in Kobi by Shigeru Ban.

81 Simón Vélez, Prototype, ZERI pavilion erected in Manizales, Colombia, 1999.

Case Study

2.1 View from the expo cable car

2.2 Exterior with sectional timber queue shelter

2.3 Exterior

Japan Pavilion, Expo 2000, Hanover, Germany

The Japanese architect Shigeru Ban has been involved in the task of designing buildings made from recycled components since creating temporary shelters which used paper tubes to form the main structural walls in the wake of the Kobi earthquake. The system has now been developed into a family of products capable of integration into the construction of larger buildings with a wide range of uses. Expo architecture always provides a particular conundrum for designers – how to create a building of significant quality which will represent its sponsors well but which will not be wasted when the show is over six months later. For the Japan Pavilion at Expo 2000 in Hanover, Germany, Shigeru Ban collaborated with German structural engineer Frei Otto and British engineering consultants Buro Happold to make a building that considered seriously the expo theme of 'Humankind-Nature-Technology' by being as far as possible constructed from recyclable sustainable material. Construction was by the European branch of Japanese construction firm Takenaka. The 72 metre long, undulating, three-humped linear dome of the main hall was a hybrid structure that incorporated paper tubes made from recycled paper sourced in Germany, timber and wire cables. The roof membrane was a water- and fire-proofed recyclable paper membrane specially developed in Japan for this building, though an additional PVC membrane also had to be incorporated to reinforce fire protection. The foundation was made from a steel frame and scaffolding boards filled with sand, minimising the conventional use of non-recyclable concrete. Internally recycled glass tiles and a paper carpet were incorporated into the finishes and the office was accommodated in a reusable steel container. This building was intriguing from the outside because of its undulating hill-like form, but inside it was remarkable – the even light that penetrated the twin membrane illuminated a continuous, multilayered, structural skin of natural materials that were simultaneously complex and repetitive. This large hall was uniquely defined by the shape of its roof and conveyed the feeling of being in a space reminiscent of a woodland grove but also, perhaps, of being inside the skin of an animal.

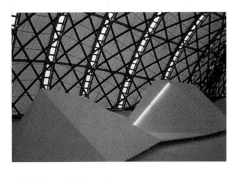

2.4, 2.5 and 2.6 Interior

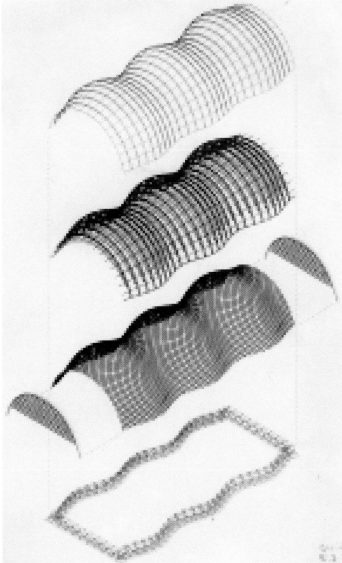

2.7 Exploded axonometric

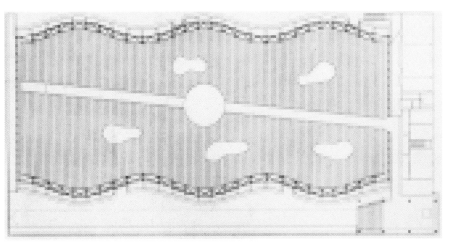

2.8 Ground floor plan

75

Simón Vélez is a South American architect based in Colombia who has become famous for his consummate understanding of bamboo, a natural traditional building material that has been raised in his hands to perform dramatic contemporary architectural tasks. Bamboo, or 'giant grass', grows naturally in many climates. In its first year it can reach a length of fifteen metres and it eventually reaches maximum structural strength in just three years. Vélez first explored bamboo for its qualities of cheapness and availability but after numerous experiments has realised its potential as a viable ecologically sensitive alternative in numerous structural and constructional applications. By combining it with small amounts of conventional materials such as steel and concrete he has unleashed its industrial building potential. His most ambitious and most visible project has been the pavilion for the ZERI (Zero Emissions Research Initiative) Foundation at Hanover EXPO 2000 in Germany. This giant natural mushroom of building uses traditional structural strategies and materials merged with new avant-garde jointing techniques, and was one of the few buildings (also including Shigeru Ban's paper-based pavilion) to respond to the ecological theme of the event 'Man, Nature and Technology'. Despite this, the German technical authorities were so sceptical of the capabilities of the system that, prior to building, a a complete full-size version of the building had to be built in Colombia for testing.

The remarkable thing about the building types that have resulted from these new construction methods is that they express their new technology in the same way as the characteristic tectonic architecture – it is not used to covertly replace traditional materials, but to make possible a new architectural form. They are expressive not only of new technology but a new agenda which states that the new is not always inorganic.

An architecture that is appropriate for our changing needs is as important now as it has ever been, but in a world that has so many conflicting messages, how do we recognise what that architecture should be like? In order to do this we need to assess how technology will impact the built environment in the future. What new technologies are available or are becoming available? How will they change the way we design buildings in the future? Perhaps more important, what will we want from the buildings of tomorrow? Until we can come to grips with these issues, our understanding of the potential of new technologies to improve architectural design is incomplete. One clue is that technological advances in architecture tend to follow behind other fields because it relies on spinoffs rather than dedicated blue sky research – so, if we look carefully, perhaps even in the dustbin of cast-off products, the technology that will create the buildings of tomorrow may already be here.

Notes

1. All analysis of this type can be criticised regarding its objectivity. The human associations with architecture examined in Part I are undeniably subjective, as indeed is any analysis based on historical, aesthetic, scientific or philosophical grounds. These arguments are therefore put forward not as fact, but to stimulate opinion, a growing awareness of the issues, and as a more substantial platform from which to develop relevant conclusions about the impact of architectural design.
2. Part of point eleven of the Futurist Manifesto of 1909. See Kenneth Frampton, *Modern Architecture: A Critical History*, Thames and Hudson, London (3rd edn.) 1992, pp.84–85.
3. Antonio Sant'Elia; from a preface to the first exhibition of the *Nuove Tendenze* group *Messaggio* in 1914 where he showed his drawings for the *Città Nuova. Ibid.*, p.87.

4. Norman Bel Geddes, Horizons, Boston, 1932 (reproduced, New York, 1977, p.24; as quoted in Dell Upton, *Architecture in the United States*, Oxford University Press, Oxford and New York, 1998, p.175.
5. David Watkin comments: 'In Italy the desire of the Futurists for violence and danger was more than fulfilled in the course of the First World War, and the country returned, like Scandinavia, to a fresh neoclassical style.' David Watkin, *History of Western Architecture*, Barrie & Jenkins, London, 1986, p.546.
6. Barbara Baer Capitman, *Deco Delights*, E. P. Dutton: New York, 1988, p.42. The quote continues: 'It was both a dime-store style, when even that mode of retailing was new, and a New York style seen at the most exclusive shops on Fifth Avenue. It was the style of the great modern skyscrapers in cities across the country [USA], yet it was also the style of the gas stations, diners, and motels that developed from the surge of Americans travelling by car.'
7. Walter Gropius, *The New Architecture of the Bauhaus*, Faber, London, 1935, p.20.
8. Angela Schönberger, *Raymond Loewy: Pioneer of American Industrial Design*, Prestel, Munich, 1990, p.96.
9. Rand's book was published in 1934; the film was directed by King Vidor.
10. Some pop architecture is technologically advanced as well, for example, the Chrysler Building was the tallest in the world for a short time when first built. As already stated, these themes are not exclusive in that some buildings will exhibit characteristics from more than one area.
11. See André Corboz, 'Modern Architecture and the Japanese Tradition', in Tomoya Masuda and Henri Stirlin (eds), *Japan*, Architecture of the World series, Benedikt Taschen, Lausanne, n.d.
12. Herman Muthesias, *Das Englische Haus* (The English House), 3 vols, 2nd edn., 1908; translated from the German by Janet Seligman, 1st English edn., 1 vol., London, 1979. *The Studio* magazine was published in London from 1886. Other influential journals were the *Architectural Review* (London), *Dekorative Kunst* (Germany), *Deutsche Kunst und Dekoration* (Germany).
13. Colin St John Wilson states that the work of the architects Butterfield, Street, Waterhouse, Shaw, Mackintosh, Webb and Lethaby, communicated through articles by Muthesias and Loos, resulted in '... the one moment in British architectural history that made an original contribution to the course of architecture on an international scale; and, if the claims of Muthesias are taken into account, it is the theoretical foundation of the Modern Movement.' Colin St John Wilson, *The Other Tradition of Modern Architecture*, Academy, London, 1995, p.73.
14. Adolf Loos, *Arkitecture*, 1910, in Benedetto Gravagnuolo, *Adolf Loos* (Idea Books, Milan,1982), translated from the Italian by C.H. Evans, Art Data, London, 1995, p.27.
15. Adolf Loos, *Ornament und Verbrechen* (1908) in B. Gravagnuolo, *Adolf Loos*, Idea Books, Milan, p. 79. Watkin suggests this piece was strongly influenced by Louis Sullivan's 1892 essay *Ornament in Architecture* which Loos may have read during his visit to the USA in 1893. Sullivan is discussed in the next section, Organic Architecture. See D. Watkin, *A History of Western Architecture*, Barrie & Jenkins, London, 1986, p.520. As well as the 1920 translation and publication of *Ornament und Verbrechen*, Loos' work was shown at the *Salon d'Automne* in Paris in 1923.
16. Adolf Loos, *Heimatkunst* (1914) in B. Gravagnuolo, *Adolf Loos*, Idea Books, Milan, 1982, p.22.
17. This statement is taken from Loos' report on the project published in 1923. Ibid., p.174.
18. Mies was director of the department of architecture at the Illinois Institute of Technology from 1939 to 1959. See K. Frampton, *Modern Architecture*, Thames and Hudson, London, 1992, p.232.
19. In some cases in the original building, painted plaster was used instead of stone for economy. The replica, built with Mies' collaboration, incorporates the materials from the original specification.
20. Kenneth Frampton describes Mies' Crown Hall, the architecture school at the Illinois Institute of Technology, Chicago, 1950-6, as a 'typical suppression of all that was programmatically incompatible with the monumental ...'. Frampton, *Modern Architecture*, p.237. Of Mies' Berlin National Gallery, Colin St John Wilson states: '...the driving force was a preoccupation with the technology of steel construction and the extent to which through *mimesis* it could evoke the form of the Classical temple. Set against the true purposes for which the building was commissioned, the irrelevance and internal contradictions latent in such preoccupations are brutally revealed.' St John Wilson, *The Other Tradition*, p.93.
21. *Tadao Ando*, Architectural Monograph 15, London, 1990.
22. Tadao Ando, 'Towards New Horizons in Architecture' (1991) in K. Nesbitt, *Theorizing a New Agenda for Architecture,* Princeton Architectural Press, New York, 1996, p.460.
23. Though to be fair to Mies' design, it is the flexibility of the steel frame and the repetitive grid that have enabled these alterations to be implemented.
24. See K. Frampton, *Modern Architecture*, Thames and Hudson, London, 1992, pp.90-91.

25 Eugene Viollet-le-Duc, *Entretiens sur l'architecture* (1858–72). See K. Frampton, *Modern Architecture*, Thames and Hudson, London, 1992, p.64.
26 Others were the Flemish Victor Horta and Henry van der Velde in Belgium and the Catalan Antonio Gaudí in Spain.
27 As quoted in K. Frampton, *Modern Architecture*, Thames and Hudson, London, 1992, p.51.
28 As well as the Secessionists, Wright would have been familiar with the work of Charles Rennie Mackintosh through *Studio* magazine.
29 Frank Lloyd Wright, *The Natural House*, Mentor, New York, 1963, p.55.
30 The italics here are Wright's.
31 Adolf Loos, *Trotzdem* (*In Spite of All*), (essays, 1897-1900), Innsbruck, 1931, in B. Gravagnuolo, *Adolf Loos*, Idea books, Milan, 1982, p.61.
32 Le Corbusier, *Vers une Architecture*, Editions Crés, Paris, 1923. English edn. trans. Frederick Etchells, *Towards a New Architecture*, Architectural Press, London, 1927, pp.266–68.
33 Alvar Aalto, 'The Architectural Struggle', RIBA Discourse, London, 1957; quoted in St John Wilson, *The Other Tradition of Modern Architecture,* Academy, London, 1995, p.6
34 However, Colin St John Wilson suggests that right from the beginning some of the modernist architects such as Alvar Aalto, Hugo Haering and Eileen Grey followed another tradition that engaged with plurality and client needs. Ibid. p.16.
35 Other architect engineers who developed the potential of reinforced concrete were Maillert and Luigi Nervi.
36 Frei Otto, 'The New Plurality in Architecture' in Marc M. Angelil (ed.), *On Architecture, the City, and Technology*, Association of Collegiate Schools of Architecture, Washington DC, 1990, p.14.
37 The spider's web is weight for weight much stronger than the highest tensile steel. Scientists are currently working on a process to synthesise artificially spider thread for commercial use. See Lorraine Lin, 'Studying spider webs: A new approach to structures', *Arup Journal*, January 1994, p.23.
38 Charles Jencks, 'The Battle of High-Tech: Great Buildings with Great Faults' in *Architectural Design*, 58, Nov/Dec 1988, pp.18–39. Colin Davies described the archetypal image associated with this form of architecture and its limitation thus: 'The various elements of a High-Tech building – the muscular steel structure, the smooth, impervious skin, the deliberately exposed pipes and air-ducts — are often powerfully expressive of their technical function, but the form of the complete building is often remarkably inexpressive of its intended use.' Colin Davies, *High Tech Architecture*, Thames and Hudson, London, 1988, p.9.
39 Fuller's writings are selectively compiled in *The Buckminster Fuller Reader*, ed. James Mellor, Jonathan Cape, London, 1970. The story of the Wichita House is told in Martin Pawley, *Buckminster Fuller*, Design Heroes Series, Grafton, London 1990. See also Joachim Krausse and Claud Lichtenstein, Lars Müller (eds), *Your Private Sky: R. Buckminster Fuller, Art of Design Science*, and *Your Private Sky: Discourse*,. Baden, Switzerland, 1999.
40 Eero Saarinen had co-designed the earlier Entenza House with Charles Eames and was also involved to a lesser extent on the 1948 project. In total thirteen Case Study Houses were built over two decades including projects designed by Craig Ellwood and Pierre Koenig.
41 For an overview of the Eames' life and work see Donald Albrecht et al, *The Work of Charles and Ray Eames: A Legacy of Invention*, Harry N. Abrams Inc, New York, 1997.
42 See *Cedric Price*, Architectural Association, Works II, London, 1984. Price's Fun Palace is due to be demolished in 2001 to make way for a sports centre.
43 A unique and frank insight into the development of the innovative ideas of Beaubourg and the task of making them work is given in chapter 1 of Peter Rice's inspirational book, *An Engineer Imagines*, Ellipsis, London, 1993.
44 Jonathan Glancey explores the link between the imagery of boys' comics like *The Eagle* and how they have influenced British architects to use technology as a visual reference in 'The Eagle has Landed' in *Architectural Review*, no.1037, July 1983, pp.33–37.
45 Nicholas Grimshaw in Rowan Moore (ed), *Structure, Space and Skin: The Work of Nicholas Grimshaw and Partners*, Phaidon, London, 1993, p.243.
46 Nicholas Grimshaw, ibid., p.20.
47 This project is described in detail in Peter Cook, 'The Eagle Has Landed', *Architects' Journal*, vol.178, No.43, 26 October 1983, pp.62–75.

PART 3

THE PURPOSE OF TECHNOLOGY IN ARCHITECTURE

Technology represents philosophy resolved to the most cogent argument ... if man did this, such would result. In technology man is empowered to explore and develop his own 'if' without reference to the limiting response of other preoccupied egos. Through technology alone the creative individual can of free will arrange for the continuing preservation of mankind despite individual man's self frustrating propensities.

R.Buckminster Fuller, 1947[1]

Fuller's conviction that all the world's problems are capable of being solved by the application of some unknown future technology now appears naive. However, at the time the statement was made many people would have believed it true for it was the beginning of a period when all the products of technology, at least in the general public perception, appeared to be beneficial. New technologies would extend life through improved health care and provide more leisure time through labour saving devices. Working life would be eased with the necessity for hard physical labour removed and transportation times reduced. It is perhaps surprising that Fuller felt able to make this statement even though he had been a personal witness to some of the problems technology can bring. Towards the end of the First World War he had seen the destructive power of technology during service with the US Navy where he served with the Atlantic fleet. During the Second World War, in response to a request from the British War Relief Organisation, he worked on the Dymaxion Deployment Unit (DDU), an adaptation of the agricultural produce storage silo, the Butler Bin, converted into simple, factory made shelters that mitigated housing shortage problems engendered by the extensive bombing in Europe during the Second World War.[2]

82 R. Buckminster Fuller, 4D-One-Ocean-World-Town-Plan, 1928.

83 Buckminster Fuller, Dymaxion Deployment Unit (DDU), 1940.

79

Fuller interpreted the destructive power of the war machine as a vivid example of how effective technology could be in also conquering peacetime problems and he subsequently strongly recommended the redirecting of wartime manufacturing methods towards peaceable ends. He foresaw a technology applied solely towards mitigating the problems of human existence and though today we might sceptically view this objective as unrealistic, the vision of technology as an all-pervasive, interlocking system that can be utilised for the benefit of humankind is a marvellous ambition. Instead of a series of individually developed techniques that addresses specific industrial, commercial and military problems, Fuller, and those whom he influenced, prophesied a future where technology could be a holistic tool that would be brought to bear on the human problems of shelter, food production and medicine in an integrated manner.[3] They saw technology as available to all, a beneficial instrument that could be wielded by anyone without political or social boundaries. Though technology has expanded dramatically, and its influence has been interwoven into our daily life in pervasive, subtle and intricate ways, it has most definitely not become an interlocking system. Though in some areas (in particular, computing) technological development has exceeded predictions, in other ways (for example space flight, personal transportation and robotics) its promise has simply not materialised. And despite many of the predictions about increased leisure time, high standards of comfort and health have become the reality for large sections of the world's population – it has unfortunately not become a pervasive power for the benefit of all the human race.

The contemporary application of technology is primarily dispersed in two ways – through government agencies and through commercial enterprise. Democratic governments have large disposable incomes which they wield to attempt to achieve their electoral ambitions. These can be associated with defence, infrastructure or services – all highly dependent on technology. Government policy can determine the development of technology either through its own research establishments or through the contracts it lets to fulfil its briefs. It can also influence the application of technology dramatically through legislation. For example, in many European countries the development of the mobile phone network has been profoundly influenced by governments that have perceived licensing as a revenue earner. The potential to amass massive amounts of cash for virtually no political effort has had two effects. First, there is the development and enhancement of the technical abilities of the system and the broadening of its opportunity for use by all in order to bring in the maximum return in relation to the cost of the licence. This new communications network has proven to be a valuable tool for business but also a popular domestic convenience. Second, there has been an unprecedented rush to implement this relatively new technology which impacts the whole spectrum of the way we live with comparatively little concern for health implications (do microwave emissions harm brain cells?), environmental concerns (transmitter masts can and are built almost anywhere), or operational problems (drivers losing attention in handling their vehicles, interference with critical aviation and maritime navigation systems). Mobile communications technology has dramatically affected all aspects of our society in an incredibly short time. However, its effects have not been predictable or been integrated into a carefully devised system directed towards beneficial change.

Technological advance is frequently like this – a wild card that can be good or bad. Confusingly, it is often both and by the time its advantages and disadvantages are understood it is already so well integrated into society that to change the way it is used is either too difficult or too costly. If we extrapolate this scenario to other areas of technological advance this inevitable package that combines both good and bad points is repeated. The motor car has improved personal freedom, communication and commercial growth, but it has also brought pollution, traffic congestion, death and injury through road accident, and blighted both the urban and rural environment due to road building. Television has brought entertainment, education and a new art form into the home, but, it has also intensified consumerism, media related crime, and ill health due to lack of exercise and related obesity.

Another challenge to the perception that technology is part of an integrated system is the impression that it is part of a process of progressive advance. In fact, each specific new technology follows its own independent route, and though there is a uniformity to the stages through which each passes – invention being followed by application and then implementation – sometimes it is necessary to wait for years, decades, even centuries for the benefits to reach fruition. The reasons for the delay before the worth of the technology can be established are diverse. It may be due to the need for other related systems to catch up before it can be implemented or, perhaps, for its value in a new application to be realised. However, it would seem that although a technology may lie dormant for many years it will eventually find its niche, before in its turn being replaced by something better. Technology will only be abandoned for good once something more efficient or more appropriate becomes available to replace it. This pattern is identified in M.F. Ashby's 'S' curve graph in which the vertical scale charts increase in performance and the horizontal scale charts effort – in the beginning the ratio of effort required to create an increase in performance is high but for successful technologies this rapidly improves until another technology begins to compete and eventually overtakes it. The sinuous line on this graph defines the history of a particular technology through development, expansion and consolidation to decline.[4]

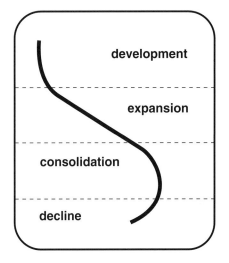

84 M.F. Ashby's 'S' curve graph.

So, if we try to describe the manifestation of technology in the world, rather than the image of a system of interlocking, mutually beneficial, continually progressing methods and techniques, a more accurate picture is of a matrix of independent developing strings of ideas that sometimes overlap, sometimes coincide, but are comparatively rarely planned to develop together. It is appropriate then that the description that a designer uses to describe the task of solving a problem is the *search* for a solution – in the vast matrix of possibilities it is indeed a search – and it is an arduous one. However, this search is important and it needs to be thorough, for if the designer is to use technology well he will need to brief himself on all the possibilities. One aspect of improved technology – Internet communication – is helping with this problem by making information access so much easier. Indeed, this resource is so huge that its very extent becomes yet another problem. In order to resolve your web search in such difficult circumstances it is necessary to know what you are looking for before you begin. It is not a matter of sorting through the solutions and finding which one will do; there are so many possible solutions that you need carefully to phrase your requirements to manufacturers, suppliers and consultants in order to obtain a limited number of close fits before picking the best. Asking the right questions is therefore the key factor in obtaining the right solution. But what are those questions? Each project throws up its own specific issues associated with function, users, appearance, environment, budget; and the way the designer approaches the briefing of these factors determines the knowledge base upon which the programme is developed.

Even before these issues of detail can be considered there is a general question that must apply to all building that is to be carried out today – in what way do we want new technology to improve architecture? The simplistic answer is to make it better – but how? In the light of past experience, which shows that the introduction of new technology has both good and bad points, the objective must be to take advantage of the benefits while mitigating as far as possible the associated problems. By deciding in advance the specific ways in which technology can aid architectural ambitions one might be able to foresee the problems and limit their impact. Planning ahead is an aspect of architectural design that is an important characteristic in the successful completion of all building projects – design teams typically have valid experience in this area and should therefore be adept at handling this issue.

In the UK the public sector is by far the biggest instigator of new building and accounts for 40% of the construction industry's annual turnover. Changes in the way in which it sets about acquiring buildings can have a profound influence on the way the industry operates and consequently on the quality of the built product. Indeed, it was concerns about the way buildings had been delivered – over budget, over time, and with built-in faults – that led to developments such as the Private Finance Initiative (PFI) which sets out to ensure 'value for money'. It is significant, however, that critics of PFI are to be found on both sides of the industry, clients and providers. The major government reports of the 1990s, Latham, *Constructing the Team* (1994), and Egan, *Rethinking Construction* (1998), have focused on how construction practice might change in response to the perceived problems of a disjointed industry and underinvestment in resources, particularly those associated with skills and technology. *Rethinking Construction* has identified five key strategic changes: committed leadership, a focus on the customer, integrated process and teams, a quality driven agenda, and a commitment to people. It has also identified strategic changes: product development, project implementation, and a partnering of the component production and supply chain which is improved by innovation resulting in integrated project processes.[5] A key factor in these new methods is the concept of 'Lean Thinking' which puts customer need at the centre of decision making rather than what is convenient for the producer – the benefits of this philosophy could extend beyond the business relationship into factors concerned with sustainability such as the elimination of waste and improved responsiveness in programme, process and solution.[6]

Though there is no doubt that change is required, the crucial factor is how the benefits of change are evaluated. The widely identified problem with PFI was that it led to anonymous, bland architecture that was primarily evaluated on capital cost rather than quality of design and sustainability issues. Achieving the specific aims outlined in *Rethinking Construction* is being monitored in comparison to Key Performance Indicators (KPIs). It is relatively easy to devise KPIs that evaluate measurable construction processes such as programming and material use; however, it is much more difficult to judge the subjective quality of architecture, its meaning for people and its long term impact in this context. Further, it is hard to imagine how such measurements can be introduced without them becoming another layer of bureaucracy to be added to planning and building control legislation.[7]

With some consideration it is possible to identify three main areas in which technology can improve architecture – the first is routinely explored during almost every building project, though for a variety of reasons the solutions found may not be the most appropriate. The economics of building are an intrinsic part of design – simply put, a project will not be built if it is too expensive. However, in too many cases build-

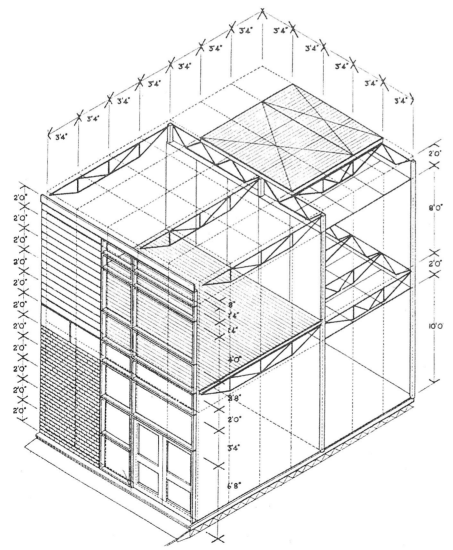

85 CLASP – one attempt to harness the economy of factory production without unduly limiting flexibility. Construction diagram from CLASP Construction 1960 *showing the vertical and horizontal modular system.*

86 The high-rise tower block Ronan Point, partially collapsed after a gas explosion in 1968. This dramatic building failure became the focus for the limitations of public housing design policy and high volume, high-rise building methods in the UK.

ing projects are compromised by an inadequate budget resulting in solutions that perform poorly. Even more unsatisfactory, the available budget may not be well used leading to the construction of a building that could have been much better if resources had been disposed more wisely. Clients of course want the best for their money, perhaps even more than their money can realistically supply. In many cases this comes down to a simple equation between the size of the floor area and the quality of the design, quality being defined not only by the materials used and the provision of services but by the less quantifiable issues of space, form and operation. The balance between quality of performance and size of accommodation can be a difficult one for clients to understand. Economy in building can be very easily evaluated by an accountant as the provision of more space for less cost, though this generally also results in a less satisfactory solution with lower standards of performance. In a competitive society building provision must of course be subject to market comparison, simple judgements based on size are easy to make, but the criteria for evaluating quality are more difficult to define. Financial cost, however, is always easy to compare, though the ultimate cost in performance, satisfaction, longevity may not become clear until after the building is in use, by which time it is often too late to do anything about it.

Clearly, using new technology can help to provide more building for less money and as this is an easily quantifiable benefit for the client, many of the technical advances in the building industry have been aimed at this objective. Componentisation and standardisation have been key technological developments in the building process and they continue to be easily quantifiable improvements that attract government research funding. System building, first made possible by the development of factory made, dimensionally coordinated building materials, makes buildings quicker to construct by reducing site work to an assembly process. When a construction component becomes cheaper (providing its performance remains the same) this is assumed to be a saving and therefore a benefit to the overall building process. However, improvements measured against cost lead to cheaper building but not better building. In a similar way, buildings that are made faster are not necessarily made better. Rather than simple economy, the objective for building improvements should be efficiency, which relates cost to quality, making more buildings with the same budget, and making them better too. Quality of building is of course not a fixed criterion. The standard of construction varies depending on the situation and location – this applies to different projects within the same geographic area; however, variations are even more pronounced from country to country. Inferior building in some localities can lead to danger to health or life, for example in harsh climates or in earthquake zones such as Turkey, where it is estimated that up to 10,000 lives could have been saved in the 1999 Turkish earthquake if houses had been built to adequate structural codes. In other poor countries which have relatively benign climates construction costs must of course be balanced against other needs – buildings may be built to a lower standard in order to prioritise spending in other areas such as infrastructure, education and health care.

The second area where new technology has a crucial role in improving architecture is becoming increasingly important as it gradually comes to be recognised as an essential factor throughout all industry. The concept of sustainable development that takes account of the impact that process has on the environment is not new. Many traditional cultures have developed techniques for using the environment to support their existence without damaging it. One example is the indigenous people of the Northwest American Pacific coast who use timber to build dwellings, artefacts and boats. However, though they use whole logs in the main structure, they do not fell trees for the planks that make up the largest portion of the dwelling, but remove portions from the living plant allowing it to continue growing.[8] The eighteenth-century development of industrial building techniques unfortunately did not create a com-

87 Pacific Northwest Indian house, Vancouver Island, British Columbia, Canada. The timber boarding is removed from the building seasonally to be transported upstream to clad an inland winter house with an identical frame.

88 Pacific Northwest Indian coastal village, Vancouver Island, British Columbia, Canada.

mensurate awareness of the impact the new processes might have on the natural environment – indeed the power of industry provided a misplaced feeling that human technology could solve any future problems while simultaneously turning a blind eye to what those problems might be. Criticism of the impact of industrial development began to emerge in the nineteenth century though this was based primarily on aesthetic and philosophical grounds rather than on a realisation that damage to the natural environment might one day become so great it might not recover. It was the religious morality of the day that identified the nobility of human labour diminished through factory work and the destruction of a natural landscape created by God, in human custody but not human ownership – a landscape that was harmed in the resourcing and processing of raw materials. John Ruskin's book *The Stones of Venice* helped establish the nineteenth-century response to art, society, morality and technology and among many arguments he described the debilitating effect that factory production techniques could have on the individual: 'You must either make a tool of the creature, or a man of him. You cannot make both. Men were not intended to work with the accuracy of tools ... . If you have that precision out of them ... you must unhumanise them.'[9] Ruskin was immensely important in drawing attention to the importance of conserving the natural world and among many others he influenced William Morris. Speaking to the Birmingham Society of Arts in 1880, Morris surely bit the hand that fed him when he said:

> *You of this great and famous town ... which has had so much to do with the Century of Commerce, your gains are obvious to all men, but the price you have paid for them is obvious to many – surely to yourselves most of all ... . Nothing can make me believe that the present condition of your Black Country yonder is an unchangeable necessity of your life and position: such miseries as this were begun and carried on in pure thoughtlessness, and a hundredth part of the energy that was spent in creating them would get rid of them ... it would soon be something more than an idle dream to hope that your pleasant midland hills and fields might begin to become pleasant again in some way or other, even without depopulating them ...*

and turning his attention north,

> *... or that those once lovely valleys of Yorkshire in the 'heavy woollen district,' with their sweeping hill-sides and noble rivers, should not need the stroke of ruin to make them once more delightful abodes of men, instead of the dogholes that the Century of Commerce has made them.*[10]

It is of interest that Morris saw the value in industry and did not suggest ridding the land of it, just mitigating its negative impact on the environment.

Contemporary building development has the potential to harm the environment in several ways: the materials used can be harmful in their sourcing, manufacture or in their future disposal when they become redundant; the energy used may be excessive in the construction of the building or in its subsequent operation; or the building process or constructional form may be inefficient in the use of materials and energy. The typical way in which building design is being improved to take account of these issues is through legislation, forcing better energy use and greater care about the characteristics of the materials used. This has had some impact in making buildings more efficient to heat and cool, and marginally reduced concern about their eventual recycling; however, it is fundamentally an add-on approach. The real route to improving the performance of buildings in terms of environmental awareness is through a fundamental shift in the way buildings are designed, setting this issue at the heart of the search for new building form.

New technology can aid this process at almost every stage. It can provide rapid computer modelling of design decisions to predict how buildings will perform environmentally – rather than over designing an artificial energy consuming environment installation, sophisticated passive systems can now be tested before the building is built to make sure they will operate as predicted. Natural lighting levels, natural ventilation, heat exchange systems can all be modelled to influence the shape of specific building forms in advance. Once installed, equipment is now commercially available that will monitor and control a building's energy use in sophisticated ways, factoring out over-heating and over-cooling and also making use of 'free' thermal resources from the occupants, machinery and solar gain. The ultimate aim is the autonomous building or perhaps even one that makes energy for other users in situations where ultimate efficiency is not possible – for example, older buildings of historic importance where physical changes to the fabric would be visually intrusive.

Material specification can now be very precise, optimising the use of industrially made materials so that the building design is frugal in their use. The range of new materials that are made more efficiently using less resources in their manufacture and implementation is also increasing. Though they may also use renewable or recycled resources, they nevertheless must fulfil the increased specification roles that environmentally aware buildings require. Tough, well drafted legislation can make an impact on the way buildings are designed. However, a better route is to access the underlying desires of clients and users by making buildings both better at the job they do and also cheaper to run.[11] When a building cost is calculated over its life cycle rather than its cost to build, ecologically sensitive solutions become much more attractive. Sustainability is not achieved solely through the construction and management process but also by planning development effectively to minimise energy use in travel by cutting down car journeys, providing effective, usable, public transport. It may also be necessary to design homes that can also be used for work, either now or as employment patterns change in the future.

The third area where technology can impact architecture is not explored in a meaningful way in the overwhelming number of buildings constructed today, and yet it contains the essence of why we build at all and continues to have a profound relevance. As explained in Part I of this study, building is an important factor in how humanity identifies its presence in the world. The making of architecture is perhaps the most profound physical act we undertake as a society – buildings may be designed and constructed by individuals but they are funded directly and indirectly by us all and they are consequently subject to our criticism and praise. It is therefore important that contemporary architecture be representative of the time and place in which it is built and as new technology is a powerful driving force in the society of today it must take its place in creating the buildings of today. Though buildings may be owned by individuals, architecture is possessed by everyone. It has always been and continues to be a symbol of its time and culture. It is the most visible, identifiable manifestation of humanity's efforts to improve its situation, either as individuals making a home or a business, or as a community, through the creation of schools, hospitals, libraries, etc.

There exist buildings which have totally negative connotations but it is significant that they are either totally anonymous, masquerade as something else, or are completely invisible. The Nazi regime created death camps and torture chambers. Subsequently there were attempts, many successful, by postwar governments to eradicate the presence of these buildings so they could be forgotten. However, their

89 *The excavated site of the former Gestapo building on the Prinz Albrecht Terrain in Berlin. Wreaths have been laid on the remains in memory of those who died there. In the top left of the photograph is a portion of the Berlin Wall and a guard post, to the right is the site where the new 'Topography of Terror' Documentation Centre will be built to a design by Peter Zumthor.*

importance as reminders of what can happen if society does not take care has led to organisations being created specifically to maintain and promote awareness of their existence and notoriety. The Swiss architect Peter Zumthor is currently engaged in the design of a new building to provide a home for a permanent exhibition that is a monument to the horrific events that took place in the SS Headquarters on the Prinz Albrecht Strasse in Berlin. This structure is the result of years of protest and debate about how and if such a commemoration should be made, yet it is important to recall that even here amidst the horror, there is the recognition of sacrifice and heroism of those who resisted the fascist regime.[12]

90 Zumthor's design constitutes an attempt to make a wholly 'honest' building in which none of the elements of structure or construction are hidden and where there is a continuous view from inside to outside and outside to in.

Virtually all building projects are intended to be improvements – even those with unattractive uses such as prisons, army camps, effluent treatment plants, are there for positive reasons. Though no one intends to build a mistake, there are of course poorly designed or constructed buildings that most would acknowledge as having failed; however, these are also a reflection of society's complexity and confusion. Indeed, the built environment parallels society in that it can be associated with so many different aspects of human needs and ambitions; architecture can have many faces – safe, comforting and stable or energetic, challenging and provocative. New technology undoubtedly accentuates the confusion but there is no doubt that it is also an ever expanding resource for the creation of a rich eclectic mix of representative architectural form. New computer-based design techniques, new materials and new structural possibilities are the obvious products of innovation, but it can also help to make buildings more accessible, more responsive, and more flexible. In this sense new technologies are part of a multiplying resource of enabling methods that can be used to create contemporary architecture. In some cases the overt image of technology in construction may express most cogently the trends of society towards its adoption and mastery, though this is just one of the ways it can mark contemporary architecture. More important is that the symbolic meaning of the building be appropriate. Regardless of what that meaning is, the technology in many cases can, and should, be invisible – passive and supportive rather than active and aggressive. As in the past, the holistic presence of the architecture is the most important thing; contemporary technology is just a remarkably powerful new tool in enabling that presence to be felt.

This study began with the question: what is the role of architecture? An appropriate way to draw this investigation to a conclusion is to ask: what is the role of *technology* in architecture? As we have seen, new technology has the capabilities to change the whole character of architecture dramatically – it has even been prophesied that it can negate the need for architecture entirely. The most evocative descriptions of a new world of experience conducted within the computer generated virtual reality of cyber space have been created by the Canadian novelist William Gibson in his books *Neuromancer* (1984), *Mona Lisa Overdrive* (1988), *Count Zero* (1986), *Virtual Light* (1993) and *Idoru* (1996), which describe a complex multilayered society totally dependent on information technology. The British architectural writer Martin Pawley provocatively suggests that the future landscape of Britain may consist of

91 The Reichstag, Berlin, rooftop public gallery renovation by Foster Associates.

continuous anonymous sheds which will form plug-in points for virtual environments; instead of architecture designed on the basis of form it will be made as an efficient terminal for the receipt and dispersal of information.[13] True, the development of instantly communicated, three-dimensional cyber realities contained within a personal cell, anonymous on the outside but totally dedicated to the individual's desires on the inside, is now capable of being more than a dream of science fiction. But is that what human beings really want? Even if they do want it, could it be a viable option for human existence? Though people are individuals, humanity has a collective identity. The communal aspect of human existence is an intrinsic part of our make-up. The most important events in our lives are associated with community and family events. One cannot celebrate life alone. Technology has been predominantly a welcome and successful aspect of human development because it engages with community desires such as transportation, communication and commerce. Its main role has therefore not been to divide communities but to enhance them, its ultimate achievement to draw the world together into a global community. There have been problems with this phenomenon – the anonymity of international corporations, the abandonment of traditional cultural values for international business, the risk of environmental disaster, and the threat of local conflict having worldwide catastrophic impact due to the power of weaponry, to list but a few of the most easily recognisable. However, there are also real benefits – transparency and ease of communications, speedy availability of solutions to remote problems, the development of a global community and international responsibility.

New technology is created by human beings to serve their needs, and it therefore accentuates their natural tendencies. However, there is one important component of society that has remained much as it has done since recorded history began. Though technology changes dramatically and continuously, human beings do not. The physiological make-up of humanity is much the same today as it has been for millennia – our bodies benefit from technological advance with eyesight and hearing aids, increases in life expectancy due to enhanced medicine, diet, hygiene and living conditions, but the requirements for good health and well-being remain basically the same. We also retain our need for personal identity, a sense of belonging, and relationship to each other, the physical world and the spiritual one. The new technology we create should therefore be made to adapt to human beings, not human beings be made to adapt to it.

In architectural terms this means that many of the characteristics of the way we live are well established and have no need for change. Just because it is possible to build an anonymous box containing an Internet linked cyber reality station to replace a house does not mean that most of us will want to live there. In a more proven simile, high-rise dwellings do not suit everyone – just because we can build an air-conditioned pod 80 storeys in the sky does not mean we will all want to live there all the time. It can be convincingly argued that in fact the ultimate house has already been built, perhaps many times over, though in many different forms depending on where in the world you are. In western Europe and North America this house has a

92 The image of home.

kitchen, a bathroom, somewhere to work, somewhere to relax and somewhere to sleep. It has a garden, is temperate and comfortable. It is close to employment, secure, and is part of a community of other houses and buildings. The role of new technology is therefore not primarily to feed speculation on variations to this design, though that might still happen as a reflection of our individuality. Instead, innovative technology's real and most important role is to make this ultimate house, and the workplaces and other buildings we need, not just for those who can afford them, but available for everyone.

VERNACULAR ARCHITECTURE – HOLISTIC DESIGN

Like virtually every other aspect of contemporary life, architecture is subject to a complex abundance of influence, the result of which in design is a myriad of styles and imagery. Some of these influences are overtly controlling and relatively easily delineated – legislation, economics, function; some are liberating and challenging – image, aesthetics, and meaning. Between these polarities there is a median range of issues such as location, environment, programme, materiality, construction and structure that defines the specifics of the architecture that will be created. These issues afford a fantastic opportunity for freedom of choice and are also available for experimentation and alteration. Controlling influences are fixed at the outset and the image, aesthetics and meaning of the architecture that define its presence result from the manipulation of the immeasurably flexible factors of place and technology – it is this group of malleable alternatives that establishes the success or otherwise of a particular architectural project.

Clearly it is a difficult task to deduce exactly what is the right solution for a specific problem, a problem which may be well defined in some ways (though hardly ever all ways) but still incredibly complex. For example, design problems associated with meeting current architectural needs can be analysed, understood and catered for, but the responsible designer may also have to consider a comparatively ambiguous future and then decide if it is necessary or possible to build in flexibility. This is just

93 Industrial vernacular – timber supports in the eleventh-century salt mine, Wieliczka, Poland.

one factor among many – finding out what, then how to build is a difficult task. Despite these problems, though there are indeed many poor buildings there are also many very good ones – architecture exhibits its share of mistakes but there is also an ample history of remarkable success. Is it possible to define how success has been achieved? It could be suggested that great buildings are the result of the individual genius of a particular architect, of the team he or she assembled, of the commitment and belief of the client and the skill and ingenuity of the building team. People of genius do pervade every profession and undoubtedly in architecture some of the best buildings in the world can be assigned to their involvement, but by placing the source of success solely in the hands of rare talent we are abandoning hope for improving all architecture.

In any case, it is clear that not all great architecture is the product of individual genius. This is most evident when we examine the great achievements that can be found among the diverse examples of vernacular building. In every country in the

94 Samoan chief's hut photographed under construction in 1903.

world great examples of architecture can be seen that were built before legislation influenced building form, before international styles determined fashion, before industrial techniques were available to dictate construction economies. These buildings were made by groups of people working together within a sophisticated logistical framework that resulted in products that have not only lasted many hundreds of years, but in many cases can still be seen to fit their purpose remarkably well and be the subject of admiration from contemporary craftsmen and designers. There are many examples: North African Bedouin tents utilise a tensile membrane structure that only in the twentieth century began to be reinterpreted as a highly efficient lightweight structural form suitable for widespread exploitation in permanent building; the yurt of Central Asia is a system built production line building that uses a combination of lightweight structures and flexible cladding to cope with dramatically changing climatic conditions; a Samoan chief's hut is a geodetic dome structure that encloses maximum volume within a minimum shell type structure; the *Trulli* of Alberobella in southern Italy bypass material restrictions to create complex forms and intriguing internal spaces without structural members that can resist significant tension loads; wide span rooves in England before the advent of wrought iron and steel utilised complex, pre-manufactured timber components to create remarkable open spaces articulated by the structure that responded to strict functional parameters associated with its purpose, whether it be church or tithe barn.[14]

The technology each of these buildings incorporates involves very different techniques and materials. However, if one carefully examines these examples and the many others that can be found, a common set of characteristics can be observed which helps explain why these buildings are so good. First of all this architecture is site specific – it is so well established in its location that it seems as though it could not have been made anywhere else. The designs are attuned to the local climate, topographical conditions and the accessibility of resources. In some cases this latter might be food and water for the inhabitants, in others a source of power for the process carried on there (say, a wind or water mill). For example, the Bedouin tent is a portable shelter constructed from a woven membrane made from goat's hair which is naturally water resistant. The long, low shelter is supported on light masts and held taut by ropes fixed to anchors made from bushes buried in the sand. The building provides shade and privacy though its side walls can be lifted to allow cooling breezes to pass through. It is easily transportable to accommodate the inhabitants' pastoral lifestyle which involves moving in a set seasonal grazing pattern. Though the tent's geographic location changes, the site actually remains the same, the communal group arranging their buildings in the same layout each time the camp is established.[15]

The form of such buildings is closely related to the requirements of the users because the people who inhabit them have a direct link with those who build them – in many cases they are the people who build them. In either case the building consummately fulfils the need of its user. The yurt is another building designed for the use of nomadic peoples. This building is made from a series of components – a collapsible lattice wall, a demountable lightweight roof structure, felt mats for cladding and floor, and a carved wooden door and frame. A specialist crafts person builds each of these components separately – brought together, they make the dwelling, which through long experience, the inhabitants can assemble themselves. Like the tent, the yurt is designed to be dismantled easily for transportation; however, the climate in which it is used is very different to that experienced by the Bedouin. The Asian steppe is windy and often bitterly cold. The building form is therefore a circular cone for stability in high wind and though light is immensely strong, with a collapsible geodetic framework that provides the wall structure. The roof is composed of concentric poles slotted into a compressive ring at the top and into the upper edge of the wall frame just above a tension band. This assembly is clad in layers of felt blankets tied and fitted around the structure to compress it into a rigid monolithic form. The circular internal layout is carefully established to respond to both family hierarchies and practical considerations. The building is erected with its doorway to the south. The fire is at the

95 *Prefabricated components for the* yurt: *roof crown compression ring, radial roof beams, folding wall trellises.*

96 Tithe Barn at Great Coxwell, Berkshire.

centre of the space beneath the best structural place to locate a smoke hole, but it is also practical in a spatial way allowing all to have access to its warmth, and symbolically important as the hearth representing the centre of the home. The place of privilege is furthest from the door, where the bed is sited and where the family's prized possessions are kept. The mother and children's location is to the west and the father and workshop location is to the east. In a compact space and one that is continually disrupted for transportation a culturally ritualised plan is also a practical benefit.[16]

Though the technology utilised in vernacular architecture is deceptively simple it has been developed to a high degree of sophistication. Traditional indigenous buildings are made from the materials that are to hand and they often have a symbiotic relationship with the landscape in which they are established. The reasons for this are undoubtedly practical, transportation over long distances being costly and troublesome. However, this does not mean that trouble is not taken over the shaping and use of those materials or that inferior performance is tolerated for expediency. In the English tithe barn the great posts and beams were made from lengths of timber that could be conveniently found in mature trees so joints were developed to enable large spans and great heights. Timbers were worked close to where trees were felled, test assembled, marked for reassembly and then moved to the construction site. Though the tithe barn is a pattern of building which emerged in response to the storing and drying of hay to make straw (a functional requirement found in many parts of England), local materials fine tuned the building for its site. Clay pantiles, thatch, slate are used for rooves in different areas – clunch, brick, wattle and daub fill in the structure.[17] This principle can be extrapolated to an international scale. Across the world buildings take different forms depending on the scope and nature of the operations they contain but also depending on the materials that are available – buildings with similar functions are made from mud in East Africa, grass in the Nile delta, timber balloon frame in North America.

The form of vernacular building is also dependent on the nature and availability of construction methods – a primary factor of which is labour. Where large groups can

97 House made using boat building skills, Lake Toba, Sumatra, Indonesia.

work together to a common goal large buildings are possible; where communities are small, more intimate personal structures develop. But here technology is also critical. Technologies developed for some other activity, for example boat building, are often transferred into architectural construction. This transfer technology may also appropriate the symbolic importance of its source. Sometimes it is clearly visible, for example adopting the shape of a boat which helps provide both food and communal unity, to inform the image and consequently the meaning of the building.[18] Elsewhere it is more subtle, the influence present in details of jointing, of weather proofing, even simply in the resourcing and shaping of materials. Continuity of technology between applications and artefacts squares the circle – it engenders a feeling of control over the human-made environment and establishes a family of materials and techniques that supports a range of diverse activities. By reducing the variety of physical expression employed it simplifies people's relationship with the manufactured world.

Though vernacular architecture is based on tradition, this does not necessarily mean that its development has been halted. Like all forms of manufacture, these building techniques can change when exposed to useful advances – vernacular architecture can be responsive to technological innovation in the same way that it is responsive to technological transfer. For example, North American nineteenth-century 'balloon' frame building was a descendant of traditional framed timber joinery systems – the dramatic improvement in the speed of construction and erection compared to its antecedent largely due to the creation of a simple artefact, the machine-made nail. Where previously both joints and nails were hand made there was little advantage in the use of the more expensive material, but when from about 1790 onwards the mass-produced nail became available, followed several decades later by an improved version with a proper head and then the circular saw, the vernacular framed building process had metamorphosed into a semi-industrial hybrid.

Vernacular architecture is the most direct response to solving building requirements. Though in many cases these buildings incorporate specialist work by individual craftsmen which is comparable to that seen in contemporary construction, the involvement of users with siting, function, materials resourcing and construction is intimate. Such buildings exhibit certain characteristics with regard to their manifestation that have been removed from most people's experience of contemporary architecture.[19] Vernacular buildings therefore characterise the *intuitive* human desire and ability to make architecture and the consequence is that the architecture that emerges is shaped only by *direct influence* – concerns regarding the use, manufacture and meaning of the building by the community that builds it are the only generating factors in determining its form. This is the crucial factor that has led to a meaningful architecture in the past and continues to do so among societies that have a strong connection with their traditional roots. It is significant that this factor is directly related to the technological resources that are employed to make the buildings. However, can the same intuitive ability be used to help create equally appropriate contemporary architecture? To find this out we need to explore modern buildings to discover if in any cases similar factors may also be at work.

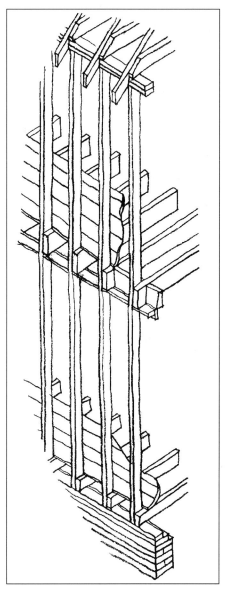

98 Balloon frame timber building construction.

ALTERNATIVE ARCHITECTURE – RESPONSIVE DESIGN

Though there are still many examples of traditional building processes in existence around the world, most contemporary architecture is created by professionals. Much of this work is carried out utilising a client/designer/builder relationship though there are many variations within this general pattern. In some cases, the search for efficiency has led to the designer becoming part of the building contract package and though there are undoubtedly some advantages to this, for example, familiarity with the contractor's building and production methods, ease of communications and simpler contract procedures, the loss of the architect as an independent advocate of the client's interests is correctly perceived by many as a major downfall of this system.[20] In many building projects the designer now has little if any contact with those who will use the building, the design role either being relegated to the production of standard plans for use on different sites irrespective of local conditions or varied users, or alternatively restricted to a limited input at an early stage in the contract and/or to the manipulation of standardised systems to provide loose-fit solutions. The direct client/builder relationship without any design input is founded on the belief that it will reduce costs, but this is not proven, and in the vast majority of cases it is certain that without dedicated design input long lasting worthwhile architecture cannot emerge.

There is, however, another form of contemporary building that, although it does not generally involve professionals of any sort, does exhibit the intuitive characteristics found in traditional architecture. The resulting buildings are not usually considered to be part of the mainstream, indeed some people, including those who have created them, may consider these structures definitively removed from conventional building practice, their aim being to create an identifiably distinct form of alternative architecture. This alternative architecture is made by creator/builders who have an intense, direct, personal knowledge of the place they wish to make. They have a holistic vision of function, image and place that is remarkably unshackled by preconceptions. Though some of their ideas may initially be quite vague this facilitates a unique embracing response to accidentally emerging architectural form that is both subjective and emotive. This in turn enables the closest of personal relationships to develop with the building as it progresses. Clearly, not having a precise view of the completed form of the building before the construction process begins is something that is anathema to the conventional building industry. This attitude is irrelevant to alternative architecture because the building users wish to take part in the building process in an intimate manner, involved in both the method and materiality of building. They are not self-builders who typically work within normal commercial design patterns in order to assure funding for their houses; however, in some cases the intuitive creator/builders do combine skills and almost always have a prime objective – to make a home for themselves to live in. These houses are wound up in complex ambitions about lifestyle and personal philosophy, as well as the more common issues of shelter and comfort. Alternative architecture is generally the product of individuals who have deeply held personal beliefs, who are fundamentally free-thinking and willing to abandon conventional hierarchies.

Individual examples of alternative development that is sited alongside but is formally distinct from the general pattern of building that surrounds it do sometimes occur. In this case such architecture is usually the result of an immensely strong-willed individual who battles against the tide. However, alternative architecture normally results from a set of specific circumstances in which a group of individuals sets out to find a place where they can live and build as they wish, or in a location where the usual rules and conventions have been suspended, unwittingly encouraging those who wish to live there to resort to alternative methods to create shelter.

99 Self-built 'plotlands' properties in 1930's Essex.

100 'Plotlands' dwellings at Pagham Beach, Sussex, made from railway carriages with customised additions.

In the 1930s on cheap coastal land in Sussex, an alternative pattern of building was established that still exists today. These seaside communities began as series of temporary beach huts, places which people would occupy during the day while enjoying the sea and the beach. Made from cast-off building materials and old vehicles – supplemented by tents when occupation spread over a few days, in time neighbourhoods developed and people were encouraged by each other's efforts at establishing habitation. The Beeching Railway Act reduced the number of local lines across the UK with the result that many older carriages became redundant. These constituted a resource for establishing more permanent dwellings, created outside the normal financial and legislative building restrictions, that have over time become a permanent settlement whose elements are individually eclectic and eccentric but together form a remarkably homogeneous alternative architectural living experience. The carriage provided a simple, relatively weather tight space which could be redeveloped internally to provide a compact living area, though conventional house plans had to be abandoned. Externally, the carriages continue to be remodelled with the

101 and 102
Self-built additions/alterations to mobile homes on the Mogollan Rim in Arizona.

patios, cottage gardens and picket fences that establish them as cared for places of personal leisure.

In the desert state of Arizona in the USA, the Mogollan Rim is a forested area at high elevation that has cool night-time temperatures and a predictable seasonal climate with long dry summers and a monsoon that arrives every July. To encourage settlement, plots were given free to those willing to commit to build a residence within five years. Many homes were originally built for vacations and began as trailers towed up to the plot and initially intended to provide a base for the annual summer building project. Rather than creating the typical mobile home community, utilising purpose built commercial buildings, the need for economy and the lack of regulations have fostered a cluster of customised dwellings, each house with its own unique character, though usually hiding somewhere under the skin is an older towing trailer. Streamlined Airstream 'Safaris', 'Overlanders', 'Tradewinds' have acquired shingle rooves, stone fireplaces, wooden porches. Surrounding plots have flagpoles, yard art and satellite dishes the size of a mini-van.

These buildings are not pretty or polite but they are energetic and individual. They use technology in an ad-hoc manner which although undisciplined is imaginative and ingenious. Such architecture is also remarkable for its predominant use of recycled material, components, second-hand building products and frequently whole vehicles such as railway carriages, caravans, buses, boats – even aircraft. Glass bottles can become translucent bricks, car door skins cladding panels, beer crates foundations. Timber, instead of always being a machined industrial product, may be used with minimal variations to its found state, each piece selected to fulfil a specific role related to its shape and strength. The selection process of materials used in alternative buildings relates strongly to the way they are employed in vernacular architecture – primarily because they are available and easily obtainable. Sometimes the material or technique used may not be ideal, but in that case it becomes temporary until a better solution comes along. This experimentation is one way in which alternative architecture differs from traditional forms; the creator/builders do not typically have the fundamental knowledge and experience of generations of traditional building to draw on. That is why these buildings are all so different, even though they may have a similar purpose and be in the same location. Each person is not only responding to an individual vision, he or she is making use of different resources.

Because the building of alternative architecture is founded on philosophical ideals rather than commercial ones it benefits from the free transference of information. In the 1920s and 1930s information was extremely localised, usually restricted within the emerging community, a pooling of skills and experience dedicated to a particular situation. In the communities that emerged in the 1960s as part of the counter culture movement the process was very similar at first; however, in a relatively short amount of time the pooling and dissemination of knowledge became more organised. The *Domebook*s were the first really successful alternative building handbooks, comparing the pragmatic details of vernacular building with the requirements of those who wished to drop out of a conventional urban lifestyle. These manuals contained a scrapbook of ideas and instructions on every type of basic construction utilising conventional materials and techniques; traditional crafts and home-made components, recycled industrial castoffs and Fuller type geodesic domes (after which the book was called) made from a wide range of material. They also printed the personal testimonies of people who had constructed their own buildings in which they recounted not only the efficacy of their building methods but also the personal experience of building for yourself. The data from the *Domebook*s were amalgamated into the single volume *Shelter* which was published internationally in the 1980s, though there were already available many other local publications that had similar intentions. Today, a similar communication process takes place, though much easier and more quickly, through the Internet.[21]

Alternative architecture is a peculiarly modern approach to intuitive building – it not only accepts the immensely complex range of industrial products of society, it

103 *'Handmade' self-built house in California illustrated in* Domebook.

responds to them by making use of the castoffs when something better arrives to replace them. The flexibility of human ingenuity is operating in two symbiotic ways: firstly in the conventional commercial world where the creation of a better product results in the redundancy of the older one; secondly in the alternative world where it is reused perhaps for a wholly different purpose. Because to creator/builders investment in human thought and labour is not a cost factor, a completely different route to making architecture can be adopted, one where the purpose and function are always in mind, but where the means of constructing the building that supports these aims is always liable to change and responsive to opportunity. Alternative architecture is created using design principles that could be described as pre-scientific; *evolutionary* development based on previous practical experience and *progressive* development during the construction process, as details and form are modified in response to trial and error. Technology is therefore perceived as a completely malleable tool and, seemingly, no matter how or of what the building is constructed the fabric will still be able to convey the highly personal image which the individual desires. This may seem at odds with the more typical professional view that in order to communicate the required image a building should be made of carefully specified materials with a meticulously calculated structure and be of a predetermined form. However, the crucial difference is that self-built alternative architecture really only has to address the needs of one person or one group. It is a highly personal, specifically tuned creation. This is why sometimes the image which the occupant may believe is comforting and domestic is perceived by others as threatening and antisocial. Even in a society which tolerates 'eccentric' behaviour the animosity expressed against those who live alternative lifestyles is almost universal.[22] Alternative architecture is the scourge of formal building procedures, it is a sign that there are other ways of doing things, outside the law, outside the mainstream – and because architecture is such an important cultural symbol it strikes at the heart of many people's perception of society.

INTUITIVE ARCHITECTURE – RELEASING CREATIVITY

Though today vernacular and alternative architecture together comprise a relatively small percentage of all the buildings in the world, the intuitive methods used in their creation still hold important lessons for the conventional client/architect/builder relationship as they can provide valuable information on how the expression of meaning and purpose through building form and fabric has emerged when people are directly involved in building for themselves.

A crucial point, though it may seem obvious, is that it is important that the architect be aware of the valuable knowledge of those intimately involved with the purpose of the building design task. This may not always be the client – the father and mother may commission a house, but what about the children who will grow up there? The factory owner may commission his new premises but what about those who make the products or who build the factory machinery? The retailer may commission his new shop premises but what about the sales people and the customers? In vernacular architecture this issue is resolved because the building forms are based on the experience and practice of past as well as current generations. It is also made easier because in many cases the lifestyle of those for whom it is built has remained relatively unchanged. In alternative architecture the design process is remarkably flexible and open ended as the creator/builder can balance out successes and failures by altering the building form as the project progresses. In conventional architecture neither of these situations applies. For this reason the preliminary investigation and brief compilation stage is absolutely crucial in determining an accurate basis for the design as the construction logistics are such that the building process is a juggernaut which cannot be diverted easily.

Though designers habitually use methods which they have acquired through education and their own experience it is important that they recognise that there are other valid methods in approaching design issues. Sometimes these are associated with religious or cultural beliefs such as the Chinese philosophy *Feng Shui* which is an established, documented design approach based on the belief that the Earth is animated by a constant energy called *chi* which can affect people's well being depending on its strength and direction of movement.[23] No doubt influenced by the ersatz versions of *Feng Shui* recently popularised in the media, most design professionals are understandably sceptical of the benefits of even this well-documented and historically persistent system – a fact which makes it easy to understand why other unofficial design approaches may be similarly disregarded. Design carried out by non-professionals may, however, access inherent human capabilities for problem solving and creativity which have become submerged beneath conventions and the dominance of specialism. Every individual has a response to architecture which is unique to them and, though perhaps less informed, is as personally valid as that of those trained in the field – it would seem irresponsible not to make use of that response in achieving the most appropriate architecture possible.

One of the most important lessons of intuitive architecture is the openness to the use of technology from other non-building fields. In vernacular architecture this occurs as a natural adoption of all the skills of the community. There is no division between the skills used to make a boat and those used to make a building, though these skills are recognised as having value and therefore as conferring special status on those who have them. In alternative architecture skills used in repairing vehicles can be used in adapting their parts for habitation purposes. In these situations it is the direct involvement with all aspects of life that makes the transference of skills and techniques so natural. In conventional industrialised building processes the possibility of using alternative technologies is fraught with problems. First, for every problem there is generally always a conventional solution available. Though this standard approach may be costly and inelegant it will have a track record, and therefore be considered a proven practice acceptable to concerned clients and the legislative authorities. Moreover, there may be an alternative solution available from other industries, which is perhaps more economical and more satisfactory in both aesthetic and practical terms, even if its use will require much research, testing, and a degree of risk taking on the part of architect, manufacturer, client and builder before it can be applied in a new role. These hurdles are difficult and costly to overcome. Proving transfer technology in the building industry is usually done on a project by project basis which means the cost of undertaking such work is borne by that contract alone. The advantages of using the new technique need to be substantial if this work is to be viable. Subsequently, if proven successful the technique can make its way through into mainstream construction as there will now exist a proven precedent. This method of introducing transfer technology can be criticised for being ad-hoc and opportunistic; nevertheless it is still perhaps the most common and therefore most important route to innovation in building design. Theoretical ideas, explored in practice, backed up with research and prototype proving, have produced some of the most important innovations in building technology in recent times, for example silicone joints, laminated timber beams and pressed metal panels.

The development of performance specifications helps the designer and the client have confidence in a new product, particularly if it is backed up by recognised testing quality control certificates such as the British Standard and the Board of Agrément. However, tests on individual products have to be backed up by authorities in procedures that replicate the product as it will be used in practice, in conjunction with other materials, components and systems. Though more disciplined, this process is an intuitive response to building, because it allows the exploration of new dedicated solutions from the innovative idea through to the proven technique and it encourages initial design to be carried out without the restrictions of relying solely on precedent.

The excuse frequently used for not using new techniques in building is the risk of failure. In his study of the achievements of the medieval and Renaissance masterbuilders Robert Mark draws attention to the considerable technical failures found in contemporary buildings, some of which are lauded as masterpieces of modern architecture. In particular he mentions the Sydney Opera House designed by Jørn Utzon with Ove Arup engineers. Begun in 1957, it did not open until 1973, nine years behind schedule and $130 million over budget, largely because of the choice of structure – a complex self-supporting concrete shell. Mark convincingly argues that the building was financially and technically a failure and that a more simple steel frame could have been hidden by roof and internal cladding to imitate a shell form. Then there is the

104 Jørn Utzon, Sydney Opera House, 1957–73.

John Hancock Building in Chicago which opened three and a half years late due to glass popping out of the windows as the structure flexed in the wind – and the Kresge Auditorium at the Massachusetts Institute of Technology whose shell roof, designed by Eero Saarinen, deformed after casting and subsequently leaked badly. Mark concludes: 'Although almost every observer would maintain that large-scale monumental architecture represents a fusion of artistic, cultural, societal, and technological motives, the role of technology in the design process is, more often than not, neglected or confused in the very treatises by which architects set great store.'[24] Later on he states '... appropriate structure should always be used for large scale buildings. I include in this category projects created primarily for visual effect, even when this leads to a literal separation of the supporting structure from the sculptural forms.'[25]

There are two arguments here. The first is that honesty in structural and constructional form is secondary to ease of fabrication – this is a debatable statement. As examined earlier, authenticity in design is a crucial factor in establishing the meaning of architecture and in determining its identity in terms of the place and time in which it is built. In addition, to find the best way, rather than the easiest and cheapest way, to make an architectural element is a primary factor in improving building construction knowledge. Without such efforts there would be no skyscrapers, suspension bridges, or auditoria. The second is indisputable: that failure is not a desirable feature of building design, though it is equally indisputable that it cannot be avoided completely. Eminent engineer Henry Petroski has a different view of failure to Mark, that it is an inevitable and valuable part of human endeavour and in his book *To Engineer is Human* he states: 'We could virtually end all risk of failure by simply declaring a moratorium on innovation, change and progress.'[26] It is, however, human nature to forget failure and remember success. Such is this characteristic that we come to expect success from all our endeavours, even when they are arduous, innovative, and at the threshold of both knowledge and experience. The questions asked in the aftermath of a great failure have a remarkable familiarity – Why did 'they' let it happen? Why did 'they' not predict such an event? It is a danger that official enquiries into disaster can be perceived as the search for blame – negligence, incompetence, malpractice or even malice. Such is the belief in human ability to avoid failure that when a TWA airliner exploded in mid-air off Coney Island, New York in July 1996 immediately terrorism was blamed, yet after years of investigation it was found that static electricity had ignited fuel vapour in the aircraft's tank.

It is in fact impossible to obviate the chance of failure in even the most simple piece of design because design in its essence necessitates predictions about the future. This is so even for the most tried and tested work – predictions are made about the standards of workmanship, strength of materials, even the type of weather that can be expected during the construction period. The complexity of these predictions is escalated for projects which involve innovation. However, it can be argued that innovation can actually help to lessen the risk of failure because when something new is to be attempted nothing can be left to chance, enhancing the designers' thoroughness, caution and care. One could go further; Richard Rogers has stated that '...

a more innovative solution would carry less risk than a mundane one because to innovate one must start from basic principles with nothing taken for granted.'[27] This is the factor that made it possible for the Empire State Building to be built to withstand the impact of a B25 bomber aircraft crashing into it in 1945, for the first mission to the Moon to succeed, and for the two ends of the Channel Tunnel to meet exactly when and where predicted. The constant search for greater technological achievement, notwithstanding the ever present possibility of failure, has connotations with the search for the sublime, as found in the spirit but also in nature – human endeavour where success is the goal also has the underlying anxiety of failure. As Dell Upton comments when discussing the nineteenth-century North American bridge builders: 'The undertone of fear, the possibility that a bridge might fall or a dam might break, made it the more admirable when it did not.'[28]

The most recent architectural 'failure' has been the millennium footbridge across the River Thames, designed by architect Norman Foster, the sculptor Anthony Caro and engineers Ove Arup. On opening day more than 100,000 people, ten times the design load, trooped on to the bridge to find that the structure, which used a new linear tensioning system to negate the need for suspension towers or compression piers, swayed in time with their footsteps. Much was made of the omission by the designers to take into account an academic paper written a few years before that drew attention to the possibility of pedestrian induced ocillations in bridge structures. Perhaps a more relevant piece of prior knowledge they could have accessed would have been the fact that in 1987, on the anniversary of the opening day of the Golden Gate Bridge in San Francisco, 250,000 pedestrians crowded across, flattening out the centre span and causing hanger cables to slacken off as the deck swung from side to side in the 40 mile per hour winds. The bridge was tested far beyond its intended design loads and the unpredicted movement caused major concern to the engineers observing from the bank. What was at fault in London in 2000 was not the predictions of the designers about the way the bridge would react under design load, but their underestimation of the huge popularity of their creation and consequently the extreme load it would have to take on opening day.

Though failures are undoubted tragedies if loss of life is concerned, they are also undoubted benefits in providing valuable limit testing experience. It is essential, however, that that experience is assessed and communicated – covering up the causes of failure, as is sometimes done in the cause of 'public confidence', is not only misleading, it is criminally negligent. Full and frank public knowledge of the true causes of technical failure is essential to ensure such disaster is not repeated. The most visible and potent example of technological failure that has ever occurred was perhaps the explosion of the Space Shuttle *Challenger* on the morning of 28 January 1986. Among the crew was Christine McAuliffe, an attractive young school teacher who had been given the opportunity to live out the dream of being the first civilian in space. The fault was traced to a faulty joint called an 'O' ring that had become brittle due to cold – there had even been a prior report suspecting the fallibility of this component. At that moment the human tragedy brought on by this technical failure overshadowed

105 *Space Shuttle* Challenger *disaster, 28 January 1986.*

the whole future of space flight. However, to abandon the future because of further potential danger to human life is unthinkable, so in October 1998, John Glenn at 77 became the oldest person to travel in space in an event which did not erase the earlier failure but assuaged the memory with a degree of success. We can confidently predict (though it is only a prediction) that because of the publicity attached to its failure the Space Shuttle's 'O' ring will never fail again. As Petroski so perceptively observes: 'While the curse of human nature appears to be to make mistakes, its determination appears to be to succeed.'[29]

One designer who has been mentioned regularly throughout this book has consistently exhibited an intuitive approach to making building forms, engineer Frei Otto. Otto's teenage years were spent flying gliders in Germany before the Second World War. These aircraft were among the most advanced flying machines of the day, ultra-lightweight innovative structures tuned by both practical experience and scientific research but manifesting as incredibly beautiful man-made objects. After the war Otto studied engineering, wrote his doctoral thesis on lightweight tension structures and then began a career designing, making and researching membranes, cable net and shell structures. Though Otto's building structures can be associated with both traditional tent building forms and organic forms found in nature they are truly technically innovative, pushing back the boundaries of what contemporary materials can do but also inspirational in the search for new materials in order to fulfil the potential of structural and spatial theories. The result is a completely innovative building technology that has only passed into common use in the last few decades and whose potential is yet to be fully realised. Tensile architecture can be expressive of a beautiful timeless natural form though with new high performance materials manufactured using fibres, plastics and foils it is reaching towards architectural horizons that have still to be charted. One particularly exciting area of research is into buildings that utilise structures which gain their rigidity by the use of tensile membranes made stiff by air pressure. Simple air-beams and low-pressure domes have found limited use since the middle of the twentieth century, but an indication of the future of this sort of building may be seen in Festo's 'Airtecture' hall, which uses air supported elements not only as beams, but as columns, walls and transparent 'windows' in an integrated computer controlled air pressure system that allows the entire structure to respond automatically to its environment.

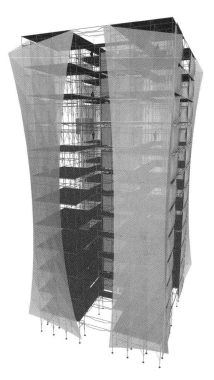

106 Intuitive architecture – a revolutionary form of tensile architecture in a design for a temporary fabric skyscraper by FTL Happold, New York. The proposal incorporates only reusable elements from the construction and entertainment industries for the assembly of the building, which is clad in a twin layer fabric membrane with gas-filled foil pillows as windows.

Intuitive architecture stems from the core of human creativity that is recognisable in the experimental imaginative play of children. A child's willingness to learn, to be open to new ideas, to disregard preconceptions, are essential components of creativity, and creativity is essential if we are to build an architecture that is responsive to the world's changing situation. Most societies have now evolved to a stage where people's occupations are specialised, and our designers are professionals having undergone a training process which necessarily attempts to respond to complex technical and cultural pressures. However, it is important that we remain in contact with our intuitive sense, because with that we can stay in contact not only with the excitement of the creative dreams of our own childhood, but also with the residual

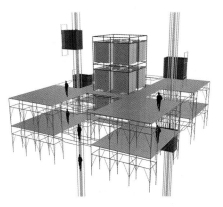

107 Temporary fabric skyscraper – section showing the structure and service elements.

Case Study

3.1 'Y' shaped columns and pneumatic muscles

3.2 Exterior front

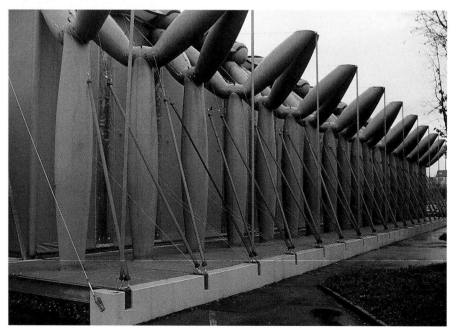

3.3 Exterior side

3 Festo 'Airtecture' Hall, Esslingen, Germany
The Festo 'Airtecture' hall is a unique piece of architecture since rather than to solve a building function requirement, it has been designed primarily to explore a technological research agenda concerned with advanced air-supported construction techniques. In pursuing this agenda the designers have developed not only a series of related new building components and an innovative approach to building control and operation but they have also created a dynamic new architectural image. Festo KG is an international company that designs and manufactures the components used to control and operate machinery in a wide range of industries, one of their main products being the high pressure pneumatic systems that power industrial robots. Axel Thallemer heads their corporate design division which is charged with creating new products associated with the company's area of expertise. Though Thallemer was originally trained as an architect he has also worked on the design of racing cars, hot air balloons, an inflated flying wing aircraft and the pneumatic muscle – a linear tube that is shortened or lengthened by injecting or removing air. The 'Airtecture' building consists of a multi-functional hall, primarily used for exhibitions, presentations and training, that is a full-sized exhibit of the company's skills. The first element of structure completed for this building was the 6-metre high, 'Y' shaped column, sixty of which effectively form the compression element for a tensile exoskeleton which also includes vertical and diagonal pneumatic muscles. The roof is supported by air beams and the walls are double skinned, air-filled panels with twin polyamide membranes maintained 200 mm apart by 72,000 interwoven threads per square metre. A transparent elastomer membrane has been developed to allow natural light into the building and these envelopes operate at a partial vacuum to maintain rigidity. Though passive air-supported structures have been built before, 'Airtecture' is different because the structure is active. The performance of the building in varying wind, rain and snow loading conditions is constantly monitored by its own computer and the building's rigidity can be instantly changed by varying air pressures within the pneumatic muscles. The exterior of the hall is robust and exuberant, its structural form unfamiliar but easy to understand. Inside the space is simple, almost bland, in keeping with its multi-functional role, though the almost subliminal clicking and tiny movements in the membrane as the air pressures are altered remind the inhabitant that this building is quite different from any other.

3.4 Interior

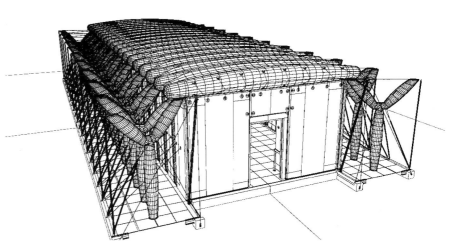
3.5 Perspective drawing

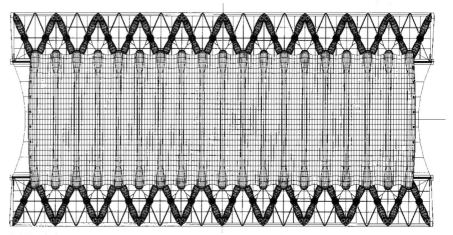
3.6 Roof plan

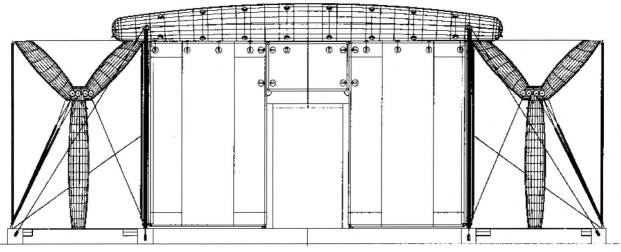
3.7 Section

108 Child's play.

creativity that all people possess. The role of architects is to express the needs and desires of all society made relevant by maintaining contact with a shared sense of human experience. If they do this, instead of being regarded as arrogant professionals imposing irrelevant ego trips on those outside 'the club', they can be recognised as sensitive cultivators of humanity's common ambitions. This is not to say that all new architecture should be homogeneous pattern making that meets with majority approval, rather that it should connect with the meaning and image that derive from its purpose and its making. The individualism of the architect is especially important as an antidote to the social control which can be exerted by big commercial organisations and governments. Perhaps this is ultimately the designer's most important role – to maintain the superiority of human sensitivity over finance and bureaucracy.

As people struggle to come to terms with changes in society, culture and technology, contemporary architecture is a sign of where we are now and an important stimulant for debate about where we are headed. It can also be very useful and, on occasion extremely beautiful! These are the definitive ambitions for a quality building, and success or failure, as with so many things, is governed primarily by human characteristics – it takes sensitivity, skill, persistence, and determination on the part of all the concerned parties to make good architecture. In the achievement of this objective, it would be wrong to regard technology as merely the means to an end. Building technology is the architect's palette and, like an artist, he or she must know implicitly how the mediums and pigments, bases and platforms perform together in order to produce a work that not only succeeds technically but is also inspired by the potential of the materials.

Architecture is an intrinsic component of the way people identify their presence in the world. However, its meaning in this context is frequently overlooked in deference to its role as an expedient tool. Most contemporary architecture utilises technology in a haphazard manner and one of the results of this is the confusion of architectural 'styles' that are adopted regardless of function or geographic location. The relationship between occupant, environment and resources that has been the fundamental balance of many of the most successful buildings of the past is all but lost in international 'no-place' architecture. Many people, not without cause, feel that advances in technology are a root cause of the proliferation of the anonymous environment. Some have therefore suggested that the solution is to return to simple traditional building methods and craftsman-based design methods. This, however, ignores the irreversible impact that technological innovation has on society and cannot be the basis for any widespread, long-term solution.

Nevertheless, the building industry compares unfavourably to other areas of human activity where technology has been used in an integrated manner closely related to clearly and sensitively defined objectives. Recent technological innovations in the construction process have been incorporated primarily as grafted-on elements to existing building methods – in many cases the ultimate goals of building provision remain short term with success often evaluated in terms of economic return. Predictions about the future of the building industry are based on situations that already exist in more advanced manufacturing scenarios such as aerospace and product design. They describe a design process that will be based on a holistic, three-dimensional entity that is a hyper-realistic model which not only describes materials' form and space but incorporates the dimensions of cost and time. The construction process will incorporate automatic procedures, robot builders and materials designed at the sub-atomic level by physicists, chemists and biologists.[30] Technological advance is an integral factor in the development of building design that, if utilised in an appropriate way, can lead to more economic, sensitive, beautiful architectural forms. In order to be exploited fully, new techniques need to be implemented in a comprehensive and holistic manner in association with research and evaluation programmes that recognise the long-term social consequences of building and environmental design. However, investing money into a specific area of research does not guarantee that it will be a success, but no investment will guarantee that nothing at all will happen in that particular area of research. Choosing where to spend money and where to do research today therefore undeniably determines what will happen tomorrow. Some buildings have been built (for example, Peabody Trust's Murray Grove housing project, the Japan Pavilion at Expo 2000, and the Festo 'Airtecture' hall) which can be described as being genuinely experimental. They are proof that there exists the potential for a truly integrated design and construction process that takes advantage of technological developments while remaining sensitive to human requirements. However, in an industry which is primarily concerned with the creation of the one-off object, it is not yet proven that the lessons learnt from these experiences will be widely implemented.

In the 1970s, Boston Institute's eminent futurologist, Herman Kahn, was commissioned by the French government to assess the country's position in a table indicating the latent potential of each member of the EEC. Kahn's methodology was briefly to visit every major European city, staying in the top floor VIP suite of the best hotel in order to count the tower cranes visible from his window.[31] In today's twenty-first century world of teleworking, out of town shopping and information technology industries, would he be able to rely on the same method? On a similar theme, Henry Petroski has no hesitation in describing the massive constructional undertaking of the railway as the great metaphor of the Industrial Revolution.[32] This inspires the question: what is the metaphor for the cyber revolution? It could be the World Wide Web, an as yet untamed resource for both communication and information retrieval that is simultaneously immensely powerful yet ephemeral and incorporeal. We have entered an age where the physical act of making something is no longer the final proof of significant change.

It is a paradox that though the results of technological change are usually profound and often dramatic, the basic requirements of the human beings who generate that change are not. In fact the intangible transience at the heart of the information age makes the need for the physical substance of architecture even more important.[33] The primary principles of security, comfort, and beauty remain the core elements of architectural design. The nature of these timeless elements does not need to be revolutionised – change is only necessary to ensure their recognition and integration into a building strategy that utilises appropriate resources in a manner that ensures architectural meaning and cultural continuity.

109 and 110
St. Louis Arch, Eero Saarinen – a physical technological symbol that embodies human ambitions, presence and beauty.

Notes

1 Buckminster Fuller, 'Earth Inc.' (1947) in J. Mellor, *The Buckminster Fuller Reader,* Jonathan Cape, London, 1970, p.231. On the same theme, Fuller stated that: '... all the deficiencies of human society and all the dangers it feared, could be overcome, resolved and miniaturised into a vast and seamless man-made service technology.' See M. Pawley, *Buckminster Fuller*, Grafton, 1990, p.174.
2 Despite Fuller's undoubted influence, his domestic scale shelter projects were not nearly as successful as the Nissen hut, or its US counterpart the Quonset hut, which were manufactured in hundreds of thousands all over the world from 1917 onwards.
3 The list of influential architects and designers, including Richard Rogers, Norman Foster and Nicholas Grimshaw, who acknowledge Fuller's influence is remarkable. Grimshaw considers Fuller a 'staggering philosopher' and describes the pride he felt in showing Fuller an early project he had designed in 1967. See R. Moore, *Structure, Space and Skin*, Phaidon, London, 1993, p.12.
4 See M.F. Ashby, *Materials Selection in Mechanical Design*, Pergamon Press, Oxford, 1992.
5 *Rethinking Construction: The Report of the Construction Task Force*, Department of the Environment, Transport and the Regions, London, 1998 (also see *www.rethinkingconstruction.org*). See also the booklet produced by the Royal Institute of British Architects, *Architects and the Changing Construction Industry*, RIBA, London, 2000 (also available at *www.architecture.com*).
6 See James P. Womack and Daniel T. Jones, *Lean Thinking*, Touchstone, London, 1997. Also see the Lean Construction Institute web site at *www.leanconstruction.org*.
7 The Key Performance Indicators have been devised by Movement for Innovation (M4I) and are outlined in detail on their web site at *www.m4i.org.uk*.
8 A detailed summary of the timber harvesting strategies and constructional techniques of the Nootka, Haida and other indians of the Northwest coast of America is given in Enrico Guidoni, *Primitive Architecture* (History of World Architecture series), Faber and Faber, London, 1987, pp.112–121.
9 John Ruskin, 'The Nature of Gothic' in *The Stones of Venice* (1853) in *Victorian Prose and Poetry*, ed. L. Trilling and H. Bloom, Oxford University Press, Oxford and new York, 1973, p.178. John Farmer in his book *Green Shift* states that '... in Ruskin we first meet ways of thinking that are recognisably ecological.' *Green Shift: Changing Attitudes in Architecture to the Natural World* (2nd edn.), edited by Kenneth Richardson, Architecture Press, Oxford, 1999, p.49.
10 William Morris, 'The Beauty of Life', text of a lecture given to the Birmingham Society of Arts and School of Design, 18 February 1880 in *Victorian Prose and Poetry*, ed. L. Trilling and H. Bloom, Oxford University Press, Oxford and New York, 1973, p.298.
11 See the Department of the Environment, Transport and the Regions, *A Guide to Green Construction for Government Estates*, London, 1999.
12 See Reinhard Rürup (ed.), *Topography of Terror* (translated from the German by Werner T. Angress), 9th edn., Verlag Willmuth Arenhövel, Berlin, 2000.
13 Martin Pawley, *Terminal Architecture*, Reaktion Books, London, 1998.
14 The wide variety of traditional building types still in active use around the world is remarkable. The *Encyclopaedia of Vernacular Architecture of the World* (ed. Paul Oliver) runs to three volumes and 2,780 images, 2,500 pages, cataloguing existing traditional building patterns still in use around the globe.
15 For an overview of the manner in which nomads relate to geographic location see chapter 1 of the author's book *Houses in Motion: The Genesis, History and Development of the Portable Building*, Academy Editions, London, 1995.
16 For more detailed information on the yurt see E. Guidoni, *Primitive Architecture*, Faber and Faber, London, 1987, p.39.
17 Tithe barns are among the wide span timber buildings examined in R.W. Brunskill, *Timber Building in Britain*, Victor Gollanz, London, 1985.
18 See Ronald Lewcock and Gerard Brans, 'The Boat as an Architectural Symbol' in Paul Oliver (ed.), *Shelter, Sign and Symbol*, Barrie & Jenkins, London, 1975.
19 John Farmer also notes the reinvestigation of vernacular architecture (though he prefers the term 'folk') as a resource for sustainable building strategies. J.Farmer, *Green Shift*, Architectural Press, London, 1999, p.15.
20 The value of UK building work that was designed by architects in the first quarter of 2000 was nearly £20 billion (adjusted to 1995 prices). Of this housing accounted for £6.5 billion. There are no statistics for how much work is done without architects but David Birkbeck, chief executive of Architects in Housing, estimates that only one in five houses is designed by architects. See Naomi Stungo, 'House Proud' in *RIBA Journal*, vol.107, No.8, August 2000, p.10.

21 *Domebook 1* was published in 1970, *Domebook 2* in 1971. Lloyd Khan (ed.), *Shelter*, Shelter Publications Inc., Bolinas, California, 1973 (repr. 1990). Some web site addresses are *http://www.shelterpub.com*, *ecohome.org.*, *harrisdirectory.com*, *globalpossibilities.org*, *ecology.co.uk*, *aecb.net*.
22 See Margaret Morton, 'The Architecture of Survival' in *Progressive Architecture*, August 1993, p.78.
23 *Feng Shui* has recently become popular. However, like the traditions and beliefs of other immigrant populations this form of geomancy has a longer history in the west, in particular North America, than generally thought. See D. Upton, *Architecture in the United States*, Oxford University Press, Oxford and New York, 1998, pp.108–110. At the client's request, Foster Associates' Hong Kong Shanghai Bank was laid out according to *Feng-Shui* principles, though the office has not disclosed if the principle is now a regular factor in all their design decisions!
24 Robert Mark, *Light Wind and Structure: The Mystery of the Master Builders*, MIT Press, Cambridge, Mass., 1990, p.9.
25 Ibid., p.179.
26 Henry Petroski, *To Engineer is Human*, Vintage Books, New York, 1992, p.170.
27 Richard Rogers in the catalogue for the RIBA Gallery Exhibition, *Exploring Materials: The Work of Peter Rice*, the exhibition held at the RIBA, London, 30 June to 25 August, 1992, p.41.
28 D. Upton, *Architecture in the United States*, Oxford University Press, Oxford and New York, 1998, p.167.
29 H. Petroski, *To Engineer is Human*, Vintage Books, New York, 1992, p.105.
30 Ove Arup, DEGW and IBM's predictions for the future of the building industry are summarised in John Worthington (ed.), *Reinventing the Workplace*, Architectural Press, London, 1997. In particular see Bill Southwood's essay 'Information and Communication Technology: The Impact on Buildings', ibid., pp.97–101.
31 France, predictably, came top – Britain, equally predictably – bottom! This story is recounted in Timothy Battle, 'Building Terms – Co-ordinating the Fragmented Sectors of the Building Industry', Ibid p.142.
32 H. Petroski, *To Engineer is Human*, Vintage Books, New York, 1992, p.61.
33 Otto Riewoldt in his 1997 book *Intelligent Spaces – Architecture for the Information Age*, calls for an architecture that returns '... to its elementary protective and identity-creating functions, to its basic role of providing accommodation, a real living environment separate from the insubstantial world of the computer.' As quoted in Loes, *The Value of Architecture*, Routledge, London and New York, 1997, p.5

SELECTED BIBLIOGRAPHY

Albrecht, Donald et al. *The Work of Charles and Ray Eames: A Legacy of Invention*, Harry N. Abrams Inc., New York, 1997.
Angelil, Marc M. (ed.). *On Architecture, the City, and Technology*, Association of Collegiate Schools of Architecture, Butterworth Architecture, Washington DC, 1990.
Armstrong, Rachel (ed.). 'Space Architecture', *Architectural Design*, vol. 70, no.2, March 2000.
Art and Power: Europe Under the Dictators 1930–45, catalogue from the exhibition organised by the Hayward Gallery, London, 26 October 1995 to 21 January 1996.
Ashby, M.F. *Materials Selection in Mechanical Design*, Pergamon Press, Oxford, 1992.
Banham, Reyner. *Theory and Design in the First Machine Age*, Architectural Press, London, 1960.
Brunskill, R.W. *Timber Building in Britain*, Victor Gollancz, London,1985.
Capitman, Barbara, Baer. *Deco Delights*, E.P. Dutton, New York, 1988.
Cedric Price, Architectural Association, Works II, London, 1984.
Cook, Peter. *Experimental Architecture*, Studio Vista, London, 1970.
Davies, Colin. *High Tech Architecture*, Thames and Hudson, London, 1988.
Department of the Environment, Transport and the Regions. *A Guide to Green Construction for Government Estates*, London, 1999.
Department of the Environment, Transport and the Regions. *Rethinking Construction: The Report of the Construction Task Force*, London, 1998.
Farmer, John. *Green Shift: Changing Attitudes in Architecture to the Natural World* (2nd edn., ed. Kenneth Richardson), Architectural Press, Oxford, 1999.
Frampton, Kenneth. *Modern Architecture: A Critical History*, World of Art series (3rd edn.),Thames and Hudson, London,1992.
Giedion, Siegfried. *Space, Time and Architecture: The Growth of a New Tradition* (5th edn., repr. 1982). Harvard University Press, Cambridge, Mass., 1967.
Goldberger, Paul. *Renzo Piano Building Workshop Buildings and Projects 1971–1989*, Rizzoli, New York, 1989.
Gravagnuolo, Benedetto. *Adolf Loos*, Idea Books, Milan,1982 (translated from the Italian by C.H. Evans, Art Data, London, 1995).
Gropius, Walter. *The New Architecture of the Bauhaus*, Faber, London,1935.
Guidoni, Enrico. *Primitive Architecture* (History of World Architecture series), Faber and Faber, London, 1987.
Hartoonian, Gevark. *Ontology of Construction: On Nihilism of Technology in Themes of Modern Architecture*, Harvard University Press, Cambridge, Mass., 1994.
Khan, Lloyd (ed.). *Shelter* (repr. 1990), Shelter Publications Inc., Bolinas, California, 1973.
Krausse, Joachim and Lichtenstein, Claud, (eds). *Your Private Sky: R. Buckminster Fuller, Art of Design Science*, and *Your Private Sky: Discourse*, Lars Müller Publishers, Baden, Switzerland, 1999.
Krell, David Farrell (ed.). *Martin Heidegger, Basic Writings*, Routledge, London, 1993 (1st published 1978).
Kronenburg, Robert. *Houses in Motion: The Genesis, History and Development of the Portable Building*, Academy Editions, London, 1995.
Kronenburg, Robert. *FTL: Softness Movement and Light*, Architectural Monograph No.48, Academy Editions, London, 1997.
Kronenburg, Robert (ed.). 'Ephemeral Architecture', *Architectural Design*, vol. 68, no. 9/10, September–October 1998.
Kronenburg, Robert (ed.). *Transportable Environments: Theory, Context, Design and Technology*, E&FN Spon, London, 1998.
Kronenburg, Robert. *Portable Architecture* (2nd edn.). Architectural Press, Oxford, 2000.
Le Corbusier, *Vers une Architecture*, Editions Crés, Paris, 1923 (English edition translated by Frederick Etchells, *Towards a New Architecture*, Architectural Press, London, 1927).
Leach, Neil (ed.). *Rethinking Architecture: A Reader in Cultural Theory*, Routledge, London and New York, 1997.
Loes, Eric. *The Value of Architecture: Context and Current Thinking*, RIBA Future Studies, London, 2000.
Lost Masterpieces, Architecture 3's series, Phaidon, London, 1999.
Lovelock, James. *Homage to Gaia: Life of an Independent Scientist*, Oxford University Press, Oxford, 2000.
Mark, Robert. *Light, Wind and Structure: The Mystery of the Master Builders*, MIT Press, Cambridge, Mass., 1990.

Masuda, Tomoya and Stirlin, Henri (eds). *Japan*, Architecture of the World Series, Benedikt Taschen, Lausanne, n.d.

Maxwell, Robert. *The Two Way Stretch: Modernism, Tradition and Innovation*, Polemics series, Academy Editions, London, 1996.

Mellor, James (ed.). *The Buckminster Fuller Reader*, Jonathan Cape, London, 1970.

Moore, Rowan (ed.). *Structure, Space and Skin: The Work of Nicholas Grimshaw and Partners*, Phaidon, London, 1993.

Muthesias, Herman. *Das Englische Haus (The English House)*, 3 vols, 2nd edn., 1908. (Translated from the German by Janet Seligman; 1st English edn., 1 vol., Crosby Lockwood Staples, London, 1979.)

Nesbitt, Kate (ed.). *Theorizing a New Agenda for Architecture: An Anthology of Architectural Theory 1965–1995*, Princeton Architectural Press, New York, 1996.

Neumann, Dietrich (ed.). *Film Architecture: Set Designs from Metropolis to Bladerunner*, Prestel, Munich, 1999.

Nye, David E. *Electrifying America: Social Meanings of a New Technology 1880–1940*, MIT Press, Cambridge, Mass., 1990.

Oliver, Paul (ed.). *Shelter, Sign and Symbol*, Barrie & Jenkins, London, 1975.

Oliver, Paul (ed.). *The Encyclopaedia of Vernacular Architecture of the World*, Cambridge University Press, Cambridge, 1997.

Pawley, Martin. *Buckminster Fuller*. Design Heroes series, Grafton, London, 1990.

Pawley, Martin. *Terminal Architecture*, Reaktion Books, London, 1998.

Petroski, Henry. *To Engineer is Human*, Vintage Books, New York, 1992.

Polledri, Paolo (ed.). *Shin Takamatsu*, Rizzoli, New York, 1993.

Rice, Peter. *An Engineer Imagines*, Ellipsis, London, 1993.

Rogers, Richard. *Towards an Urban Renaissance, Final Report of the Urban Task Force*, E&FN Spon, London, 1999.

Royal Institute of British Architects. *Architects and the Changing Construction Industry*, RIBA, London, 2000.

Rudofsky, Bernard. *Architecture without Architects*, Museum of Modern Art, New York, 1965 (University of New Mexico Press, Albuquerque, 1987).

Rürup, Reinhard (ed.). *Topography of Terror* (translated from the German by Werner T. Angress), 9th edn., Verlag Willmuth Arenhövel, Berlin, 2000.

St John Wilson, Colin. *The Other Tradition of Modern Architecture: The Uncompleted Project*, Academy, London, 1995.

Schiffer, Herbert. *Shaker Architecture*, Schiffer Publishing Ltd, West Chester, Pennsylvania, 1979.

Schönberger, Angela. *Raymond Loewy: Pioneer of American Industrial Design*, Prestel, Munich, 1990.

Tadao Ando, Architectural Monograph 15, Academy, London, 1990.

Trilling, Lionel and Bloom, Harold (eds). *Victorian Prose and Poetry*, Oxford University Press, London and New York, 1973.

Upton, Dell. *Architecture in the United States*, Oxford History of Art, Oxford University Press, Oxford and New York, 1998.

Venturi, Robert and Scott-Brown, Denise. *Complexity and Contradiction in Architecture*, Museum of Modern Art, New York, 1966.

Venturi, Robert, Scott–Brown, Denise and Izenour, Steve. *Learning from Las Vegas*, MIT Press, Cambridge, Mass., 1972 (rev. edn., 1977).

Ward-Perkins, J.B. *The Severan Buildings of Lepcis Magna: An Architectural Survey*, The Society for Libyan Studies, London, 1993.

Watkin, David. *A History of Western Architecture*, Barrie & Jenkins, London, 1986.

Womack, James P. and Jones, Daniel T. *Lean Thinking*, Touchstone, London, 1997.

Worthington, John (ed.). *Reinventing the Workplace*, Architectural Press, London, 1997.

Wright, Frank Lloyd. *The Natural House*, Mentor, New York, 1954 (this edn. 1963).

Website resources

www.aecb.net
www.ecohome.org
www.globalpossibilities.org
www.leanconstruction.org
www.peabody.org.uk
www.shelterpub.com

www.architecture.com
www.ecology.co.uk
www.harrisdirectory.com
www.m4i.org.uk
www.rethinkingconstruction.org